DRAMATIS PERSONÆ

As originally played at Covent Garden on
17th January, 1775

SIR ANTHONY ABSOLUTE	*Mr Shuter*
CAPTAIN ABSOLUTE	*Mr Woodward*
FAULKLAND	*Mr Lewis*
ACRES	*Mr Quick*
SIR LUCIUS O'TRIGGER	*Mr Lee*
FAG	*Mr Lee Lewes*
DAVID	*Mr Dunstal*
COACHMAN	*Mr Fearon*
MRS MALAPROP	*Mrs Green*
LYDIA LANGUISH	*Miss Barsanti*
JULIA	*Mrs Bulkley*
LUCY	*Mrs Lessingham*

MAID, BOY, SERVANTS, ETC.

THE SCENE: Bath
THE TIME OF ACTION: Five Hours

SYNOPSIS OF SCENES

ACT I

THE RIVALS

A Comedy

by

RICHARD BRINSLEY SHERIDAN

SAMUEL  FRENCH

LONDON
NEW YORK   TORONTO   SYDNEY   HOLLYWOOD

MADE AND PRINTED IN GREAT BRITAIN BY
LATIMER TREND & COMPANY LTD, PLYMOUTH
MADE IN ENGLAND

THE RIVALS

ACT I

SCENE I

SCENE—*A street in Bath.*

When the CURTAIN *rises, the stage is empty. The* COACHMAN *enters* L *and crosses the stage.* FAG *enters* L, *looking after him.*

FAG. What! Thomas! Sure 'tis he! (*Coming* C) What! Thomas! Thomas!

COACHMAN (*turning*) Hey! Odd's life! (*Coming* C) Mr Fag! Give us your hand, my old fellow-servant.

FAG. Excuse my glove, Thomas: I'm devilish glad to see you, my lad. Why, my prince of charioteers, you look as hearty! But who the deuce thought of seeing you in Bath?

COACHMAN. Sure, master, Madam Julia, Harry, Mrs Kate and the postilion, be all come.

FAG. Indeed!

COACHMAN. Ay! Master thought another fit of the gout was coming to make him a visit; so he'd a mind to gi't the slip, and —whip!—we were all off at an hour's warning.

FAG. Ay, ay! Hasty in everything, or it would not be Sir Anthony Absolute!

COACHMAN. But tell us, Mr Fag, how does young master? Odd! Sir Anthony will stare to see the captain here!

FAG. I do not serve Captain Absolute now.

COACHMAN. Why, sure!

FAG. At present I am employed by Ensign Beverley.

COACHMAN. I doubt, Mr Fag, you ha'n't changed for the better.

FAG. I have *not* changed, Thomas.

COACHMAN. No! Why, didn't you say you had left young master?

FAG. No. Well, honest Thomas, I must puzzle you no farther: briefly then—Captain Absolute and Ensign Beverley are one and the same person.

COACHMAN. The devil they are!

FAG. So it is indeed, Thomas; and the *ensign* half of my master being on guard at present—the *captain* has nothing to do with me.

COACHMAN. So, so! What, this is some freak, I warrant! Do tell us, Mr Fag, the meaning o't—you know I ha' trusted you.

FAG. You'll be secret, Thomas?

COACHMAN. As a coach-horse.

FAG. Why then, the cause of all this is—Love—Love, Thomas, who (as you may get read to you) has been a masquerader ever since the days of Jupiter.

COACHMAN. Ay, ay; I guess'd there was a lady in the case. But pray, why does your master pass only for *ensign*? Now if he had shamm'd *general* indeed . . .

FAG. Ah, Thomas! There lies the mystery o' the matter. Hark'ee, Thomas. My master is in love with a lady of a very singular taste: a lady who likes him better as a *half-pay ensign* than if she knew he was son and heir to Sir Anthony Absolute, a baronet of three thousand a year.

COACHMAN. That is an odd taste indeed! But has she got the stuff, Mr Fag? Is she rich, hey?

FAG. Rich! Why, I believe she owns half the stocks. Zounds! Thomas, she could pay the national debt as easily as I could my washerwoman! She has a lap-dog that eats out of gold, she feeds her parrot with small pearls, and all her thread-papers are made of bank-notes!

COACHMAN. Bravo, faith! Odd! I warrant she has a set of thousands at least; but does she draw kindly with the captain?

FAG. As fond as pigeons.

COACHMAN. May one hear her name?

FAG. Miss Lydia Languish. But there is an old tough aunt in the way; though, by the by, she has never seen my master—for we got acquainted with miss while on a visit in Gloucestershire.

COACHMAN. Well—I wish they were once harnessed together in matrimony. But pray, Mr Fag, what kind of a place is this Bath? I ha' heard a deal of it—here's a mort o' merrymaking, hey?

FAG. Pretty well, Thomas, pretty well—'tis a good lounge. In the morning we go to the pump-room (though neither my master nor I drink the waters); after breakfast we saunter on the parades, or play a game at billiards; at night we dance; but d——n the place, I'm tired of it: their regular hours stupefy me —not a fiddle nor a card after eleven! However, Mr Faulkland's gentleman and I keep it up a little in private parties; I'll introduce you there, Thomas—you'll like him much.

COACHMAN. Sure I know Mr Du Peigne—you know his master is to marry Madam Julia.

FAG. I had forgot. But, Thomas, you must polish a little— indeed you must. Here now—this wig! What the devil do you do with a wig, Thomas? None of the London whips of any degree of *ton* wear wigs now.

COACHMAN. [More's the pity! More's the pity, I say. Odd's life! When I heard how the lawyers and doctors had took to their own hair, I thought how 'twould go next. Odd rabbit it! When the fashion had got foot on the Bar, I guess'd 'twould

mount to the Box! But 'tis all out of character, believe me, Mr
Fag: and look'ee, I'll never gi' up mine—the lawyers and doctors
may do as they will.

FAG. Well, Thomas, we'll not quarrel about that.

COACHMAN. Why, bless you, the gentlemen of the professions
ben't all of a mind—for in our village now, thoff Jack Gauge,
the exciseman, has ta'en to his carrots, there's little Dick the
farrier swears he'll never forsake his bob, tho' all the college
should appear with their own heads!

FAG. Indeed! Well said, Dick!] But hold—mark! Mark,
Thomas!

COACHMAN. Zooks! 'Tis the captain. Is that the lady with him?

FAG. No! No! That is Madam Lucy—my master's mistress's
maid. They lodge at that house—but I must after him to tell
him the news.

COACHMAN. Odd! He's giving her money! Well, Mr Fag . . .

FAG. Good-bye, Thomas. I have an appointment in Gyde's
Porch this evening at eight; meet me there, and we'll make a
little party.

(*The* COACHMAN *exits* R. FAG *exits* L)

SCENE 2

SCENE—*A dressing-room in Mrs Malaprop's lodgings.*

LYDIA *is sitting* R *on a sofa* C, *with a book in her hand.* LUCY, *has
just returned from a message, stands at the* L *downstage corner of the
sofa.*

LUCY. Indeed, ma'am, I traversed half the town in search of
it: I don't believe there's a circulating library in Bath, I ha'n't
been at.

LYDIA. And could not you get *The Reward of Constancy*?

LUCY. No, indeed, ma'am.

LYDIA. Nor *The Fatal Connexion*?

LUCY. No, indeed, ma'am.

LYDIA. Nor *The Mistakes of the Heart*?

LUCY. Ma'am, as ill luck would have it, Mr Bull said Miss
Sukey Saunter has just fetched it away.

LYDIA (*rising and coming forward*) Heigh-ho! Did you inquire for
The Delicate Distress?

LUCY. Or, *The Memoirs of Lady Woodford*? Yes, indeed, ma'am.
I asked everywhere for it; and I might have brought it from Mr
Frederick's, but Lady Slattern Lounger, who had just sent it
home, had so soiled and dog's-ear'd it, it wa'nt fit for a Christian
to read.

LYDIA. Heigh-ho! Yes, I always know when Lady Slattern

has been before me. She has a most observing thumb; and, I believe, cherishes her nails for the convenience of making marginal notes. Well, child, what have you brought me?

LUCY. Oh! here, ma'am. (*Taking books from under her cloak, and from her pockets*) This is *The Gordian Knot*—and this *Peregrine Pickle*. Here are *The Tears of Sensibility*, and *Humphrey Clinker*. This is *The Memoirs of a Lady of Quality, written by herself*, and here the second volume of *The Sentimental Journey*.

LYDIA. Heigh-ho! What are those books by the glass?

LUCY (*going to the table up* L) The great one is only *The Whole Duty of Man*, where I press a few blonds, ma'am.

LYDIA. Very well—give me the *sal volatile*.

LUCY. Is it in a blue cover, ma'am?

LYDIA. My smelling-bottle, you simpleton!

LUCY. Oh, the drops! (*Coming down to Lydia*) Here, ma'am.

LYDIA. Hold! Here's someone coming—quick, see who it is.

(LUCY *exits* L)

Surely I heard my cousin Julia's voice.

(LUCY *enters* L)

LUCY. Lud! Ma'am, here is Miss Melville.

LYDIA. Is it possible.

(JULIA *enters* L. LYDIA *comes* C, *and* JULIA *comes to her*)

My dearest Julia, how delighted am I! (*Embrace*) How unexpected was this happiness!

JULIA. True, Lydia—and our pleasure is the greater——

(LYDIA *and* JULIA *sit on the sofa*)

—but what has been the matter? You were denied to me at first!

LYDIA. Ah, Julia, I have a thousand things to tell you! But first inform me what has conjured you to Bath? Is Sir Anthony here?

JULIA. He is—we are arrived within this hour—and I suppose he will be here to wait on Mrs Malaprop as soon as he is dressed.

LYDIA. Then before we are interrupted, let me impart to you some of my distress! I know your gentle nature will sympathize with me, though your prudence may condemn me! My letters have informed you of my whole connection with Beverley; but I have lost him, Julia! My aunt has discovered our intercourse by a note she intercepted, and has confined me ever since! Yet, would you believe it? She has absolutely fallen in love with a tall Irish baronet she met one night since we have been here, at Lady Macshuffle's rout.

JULIA. You jest, Lydia!

LYDIA. No, upon my word. She really carries on a kind of correspondence with him, under a feigned name though, till she chooses to be known to him; but it is a Delia or a Celia, I assure you.

JULIA. Then, surely, she is now more indulgent to her niece.

LYDIA. Quite the contrary. Since she has discovered her own frailty, she is become more suspicious of mine. Then I must inform you of another plague? (*She rises and moves a little down* R) That odious Acres is to be in Bath today; so that I protest I shall be teased out of all spirits!

JULIA. Come, come, Lydia, hope for the best—Sir Anthony shall use his interest with Mrs Malaprop.

LYDIA. But you have not heard the worst. Unfortunately I quarrelled with my poor Beverley, just before my aunt made the discovery, and I have not seen him since, to make it up.

JULIA. What was his offence?

LYDIA. Nothing at all! But, I don't know how it was, as often as we had been together, we had never had a quarrel! And somehow, I was afraid he would never give me an opportunity. So, last Thursday, I wrote a letter to myself, to inform myself that Beverley was at that time paying his addresses to another woman. I signed it "*Your friend unknown*", showed it to Beverley, charged him with his falsehood, put myself in a violent passion, and vow'd I'd never see him more.

JULIA. And you let him depart so, and have not seen him since?

LYDIA. 'Twas the next day my aunt found the matter out. I intended only to have teased him three days and a half, and now I've lost him for ever. (*She turns up stage, in tears*)

JULIA. If he is as deserving and sincere as you have represented him to me, he will never give you up so. Yet consider, Lydia, you tell me he is but an ensign, and you have thirty thousand pounds!

LYDIA (*coming down above the* R *end of the sofa*) But you know I lose most of my fortune if I marry without my aunt's consent, till of age; and that is what I have determined to do, ever since I knew the penalty. Nor could I love the man who would wish to wait a day for the alternative.

JULIA. Nay, this is caprice!

LYDIA (*coming round the* R *end of the sofa, and sitting*) What, does Julia tax me with caprice? I thought her lover Faulkland had inured her to it.

JULIA. I do not love even *his* faults.

LYDIA. But apropos—you have sent to him, I suppose?

JULIA. Not yet, upon my word—nor has he the least idea of my being in Bath. Sir Anthony's resolution was so sudden, I could not inform him of it.

LYDIA. Well, Julia, you are your own mistress (though under the protection of Sir Anthony), yet have you, for this long year, been a slave to the caprice, the whim, the jealousy of this ungrateful Faulkland, who will ever delay assuming the right of a husband, while you suffer him to be equally imperious as a lover.

JULIA. Nay, you are wrong entirely. We were contracted before my father's death. (*She rises, somewhat embarrassed, and moves a little* L) That, and some consequent embarrassments, have delayed what I know to be my Faulkland's most ardent wish. He is too generous to trifle on such a point. And for his character, you wrong him there too. No, Lydia, he is too proud, too noble to be jealous; if he is captious, 'tis without dissembling; if fretful, without rudeness. Unused to the fopperies of love, he is negligent of the little duties expected from a lover—but being unhackneyed in the passion, his affection is ardent and sincere; and as it engrosses his whole soul, he expects every thought and emotion of his mistress to move in unison with his. (*Coming to front of sofa, and sitting*) Yet, though his pride calls for his full return, his humility makes him undervalue those qualities in him which would entitle him to it; and not feeling why he should be loved to the degree he wishes, he still suspects that he is not loved enough. This temper, I must own, has cost me many unhappy hours: but I have learned to think myself his debtor, for those imperfections which arise from the ardour of his attachment.

LYDIA. Well, I cannot blame you for defending him. But tell me candidly, Julia, had he never saved your life, do you think you should have been attached to him as you are? Believe me, the rude blast that overset your boat was a prosperous gale of love to him.

JULIA. Gratitude may have strengthened my attachment to Mr Faulkland, but I loved him before he had preserved me; yet surely that alone were an obligation sufficient.

LYDIA. Obligation! Why a water-spaniel would have done as much! Well, I should never think of giving my heart to a man because he could swim.

JULIA. Come, Lydia, you are too inconsiderate.

LYDIA. Nay, I do but jest. What's here?

(LUCY *enters in a hurry, from* L)

LUCY. O, ma'am, here is Sir Anthony Absolute just come home with your aunt.

LYDIA. They'll not come here. Lucy, do you watch.

(LUCY *exits* L. LYDIA *and* JULIA *rise*)

JULIA. Yet I must go. Sir Anthony does not know I am here, and if we meet, he'll detain me, to show me the town. I'll take another opportunity of paying my respects to Mrs Malaprop, when she shall treat me, as long as she chooses, with her select words so ingeniously *misapplied*, without being *mispronounced*.

(LUCY *enters* L)

LUCY. O Lud! Ma'am, they are both coming up stairs.

LYDIA. Well, I'll not detain you, coz. Adieu, my dear Julia, I'm sure you are in haste to send to Faulkland.

(*She goes with* JULIA *to the door down* R)

There—through my room you'll find another staircase.

JULIA. Adieu!

(JULIA *embraces* LYDIA *and exits*)

LYDIA. Here, my dear Lucy, hide these books. Quick, quick. Fling *Peregrine Pickle* under the toilet——

(LUCY *puts the book under the cover of the dressing-table*)

—throw *Roderick Random* into the closet——

(LUCY *opens the door of the wardrobe* L, *and throws the book into it*)

—put *The Innocent Adultery* into *The Whole Duty of Man*—thrust *Lord Aimworth* under the sofa (*she takes the book and puts it under the sofa; and "Ovid" goes under the pillow*)—cram *Ovid* behind the bolster—there—put *The Man of Feeling* into your pocket—so, so —now lay *Mrs Chapone* in sight (*she puts it on the sofa from behind*) and leave *Fordyce's Sermons* open on the table.

LUCY. O burn it, ma'am, the hairdresser has torn away as far as *Proper Pride*.

LYDIA. Never mind—open at *Sobriety*. Fling me *Lord Chesterfield's Letters*.

(LUCY *throws the book to her,*

Now for 'em. (*She sits* R, *on the sofa*)

(LUCY *exits* L

MRS MALAPROP *and* SIR ANTHONY ABSOLUTE *enter from* L)

MRS MALAPROP. There, Sir Anthony, there sits the deliberate simpleton who wants to disgrace her family, and lavish herself on a fellow not worth a shilling.

LYDIA (*rising*) Madam, I thought you once . . .

MRS MALAPROP (*crossing to Lydia*) You thought, miss! I don't know any business you have to think at all—thought does not become a young woman. But the point we would request of you is, that you will promise to forget this fellow—to illiterate him, I say, quite from your memory.

LYDIA. Ah, madam! our memories are independent of our wills. (*Moving to* R) It is not so easy to forget.

MRS MALAPROP. But I say it is, miss; there is nothing on earth so easy as to forget, if a person chooses to set about it. (*Sitting* R, *on the sofa*) I'm sure I have as much forgot your poor dear uncle as if he had never existed and I thought it my duty so to do; and let me tell you, Lydia, these violent memories don't become a young woman.

SIR ANTHONY. Why, sure, she won't pretend to remember what she's ordered not! Ay, this comes of her reading!

LYDIA. What crime, madam, have I committed, to be treated thus?

MRS MALAPROP. Now don't attempt to extirpate yourself from this matter; you know I have proof controvertible of it. But tell me, will you promise to do as you're bid? Will you take a husband of your friends' choosing?

LYDIA. Madam, I must tell you plainly, that had I no preference for anyone else, the choice you have made would be my aversion.

MRS MALAPROP. What business have you, miss, with *preference* and *aversion*? They don't become a young woman; and you ought to know, that as both always wear off, 'tis safest in matrimony to begin with a little *aversion*. I am sure I hated your poor dear uncle before marriage as if he'd been a blackamoor—and yet, miss, you are sensible what a wife I made! And when it pleased Heaven to release me from him, 'tis unknown what tears I shed! But suppose we were going to give you another choice, will you promise to give up this Beverley?

LYDIA. Could I belie my thoughts so far as to give that promise, my actions would certainly as far belie my words.

MRS MALAPROP. Take yourself to your room. You are fit company for nothing but your own ill-humours.

LYDIA. Willingly, ma'am—I cannot change for the worse.

(LYDIA *exits* R)

MRS MALAPROP. There's a little intricate hussy for you!

SIR ANTHONY. It is not to be wondered at, ma'am, all this is the natural consequence of teaching girls to read. Had I a thousand daughters, by Heaven! I'd as soon have them taught the black art as their alphabet!

MRS MALAPROP. Nay, nay, Sir Anthony, you are an absolute misanthropy.

SIR ANTHONY (*moving up to the* R *end of the sofa*) In my way hither, Mrs Malaprop, I observed your niece's maid coming forth from a circulating library! She had a book in each hand—they were half-bound volumes, with marble covers! From that moment I guessed how full of duty I should see her mistress!

MRS MALAPROP. Those are vile places, indeed!

SIR ANTHONY. Madam, a circulating library in a town is as an evergreen tree of diabolical knowledge! It blossoms through the year! And depend on it, Mrs Malaprop, that they who are so fond of handling the leaves, will long for the fruit at last.

MRS MALAPROP. Fy, fy, Sir Anthony! You surely speak laconically.

Sir Anthony. Why, Mrs Malaprop, in moderation, now, what would you have a woman know?

Mrs Malaprop. Observe me, Sir Anthony. I would by no means wish a daughter of mine to be a progeny of learning; I don't think so much learning becomes a young woman; for instance, I would never let her meddle with Greek, or Hebrew or Algebra, or Simonry, or Fluxions, or Paradoxes, or such inflammatory branches of learning—neither would it be necessary for her to handle any of your mathematical, astronomical, diabolical instruments. But, Sir Anthony, I would send her, at nine years old, to a boarding-school, in order to learn a little ingenuity and artifice. Then, sir, she should have a supercilious knowledge in accounts; as she grew up, I would have her instructed in geometry, that she might know something of the contagious countries; but above all, Sir Anthony, she should be mistress of orthodoxy, that she might not misspell, and mispronounce words so shamefully as girls usually do; and likewise that she might reprehend the true meaning of what she is saying. This, Sir Anthony, is what I would have a woman know; and I don't think there is a superstitious article in it.

Sir Anthony. Well, well, Mrs Malaprop, I will dispute the point no further with you; though I must confess that you are a truly moderate and polite arguer, for almost every third word you say is on my side of the question. But, Mrs Malaprop, to the more important point in debate—you say you have no objection to my proposal?

Mrs Malaprop. None, I assure you. I am under no positive engagement with Mr Acres, and as Lydia is so obstinate against him, perhaps your son may have better success.

Sir Anthony (rising and moving down L) Well, madam, I will write for the boy directly. He knows not a syllable of this yet, though I have for some time had the proposal in my head. (Walking up L) He is at present with his regiment.

Mrs Malaprop. We have never seen your son, Sir Anthony; but I hope no objection on his side.

Sir Anthony (arriving level with the back of the sofa; sharply) Objection! Let him object if he dare! No, no, Mrs Malaprop, Jack knows that the least demur puts me in a frenzy directly. My process was always very simple—in their younger days, 'twas "Jack, do this"—if he demurred, I knocked him down—and if he grumbled at that, I always sent him out of the room.

Mrs Malaprop. Ay, and the properest way, o' my conscience! Nothing is so conciliating to young people as severity. Well, Sir Anthony, I shall give Mr Acres his discharge, and prepare Lydia to receive your son's invocations; and I hope you will represent her to the captain as an object not altogether illegible.

Sir Anthony (coming round to her) Madam, I will handle the subject prudently. Well, I must leave you; (taking her hand and *kissing it*) and let me beg you, Mrs Malaprop, to enforce this matter roundly to the girl; take my advice—(*turning*) keep a tight hand: if she rejects this proposal, clap her under lock and key; and if you were just to let the servants forget to bring her dinner for three or four days, you can't conceive how she'd come about.

(SIR ANTHONY *exits* L)

MRS MALAPROP (*rising*) Well, at any rate, I shall be glad to get her from under my intuition. (*Moving down* R) She has somehow discovered my partiality for Sir Lucius O'Trigger—sure, Lucy can't have betrayed me! No, the girl is such a simpleton, I should have made her confess it. (*Moving to* C) Lucy! Lucy! Had she been one of the artificial ones, I should never have trusted her.

(LUCY *enters* L)

LUCY (*moving to* LC) Did you call, ma'am?
MRS MALAPROP. Yes, girl. Did you see Sir Lucius while you was out?
LUCY. No, indeed, ma'am, not a glimpse of him.
MRS MALAPROP. You are sure, Lucy, that you never mentioned . . .
LUCY. O Gemini! I'd sooner cut my tongue out.
MRS MALAPROP. Well, don't let your simplicity be imposed on.
LUCY. No, ma'am.
MRS MALAPROP. So, come to me presently, and I'll give you another letter to Sir Lucius; but mind, Lucy—if ever you betray what you are entrusted with (unless it be other people's secrets to me), you forfeit my malevolence for ever; (*she moves to the door* L, *stops and turns to Lucy*) and your being a simpleton shall be no excuse for your locality.

(MRS MALAPROP *exits* L)

LUCY (*moving to* C) Ha! ha! ha! So my dear *simplicity*, let me give you a little respite. (*Altering her manner*) Let girls in my station be as fond as they please of appearing expert and knowing in their trusts; commend me to a mask of silliness and a pair of sharp eyes for my own interest under it! Let me see to what account have I turned my simplicity lately. (*She looks at a paper*) For *abetting Miss Lydia Languish in a design of running away with an ensign—in money, sundry times, twelve pound twelve; gowns, five; hats, ruffles, caps, etc., etc., numberless. From the said ensign, within this last month, six guineas and a half.* About a quarter's pay! Item, *from Mrs Malaprop, for betraying the young people to her*—when I found matters were likely to be discovered—*two guineas and a black padusoy.* Item, *from Mr Acres, for carrying divers letters*— which I never delivered—*two guineas and a pair of buckles.* Item, *from Sir Lucius O'Trigger, three crowns, two gold pocket-pieces, and a silver snuff-box.* Well done, *simplicity!* Yet I was forced to make my Hibernian believe that he was corresponding not with the aunt, but with the niece: for though not over rich, I found he had too much pride and delicacy to sacrifice the feelings of a gentleman to the necessities of his fortune.

(Lucy *exits* l)

ACT II

Scene—*Captain Absolute's lodgings.*

When the Curtain *rises,* Captain Absolute *is seated in the chair* R *of the fireplace, trimming his nails.* Fag *is standing beside the upstage* L *corner of the chair* L.

Fag. Sir, while I was there Sir Anthony came in: I told him you had sent me to inquire after his health, and to know if he was at leisure to see you.

Absolute. And what did he say on hearing I was at Bath?

Fag. Sir, in my life I never saw an elderly gentleman more astonished! He started back two or three paces, rapt out a dozen interjectural oaths, and asked what the devil had brought you here?

Absolute. Well, sir, and what did you say?

Fag. O, I lied, sir—I forget the precise lie; but you may depend on 't, he got no truth from me. Yet, with submission, for fear of blunders in future, I should be glad to fix what *has* brought us to Bath; in order that we may lie a little consistently. Sir Anthony's servants were curious, sir, very curious indeed.

Absolute. You have said nothing to them?

Fag. O, not a word, sir, not a word! Mr Thomas, indeed, the coachman (whom I take to be the discreetest of whips) . . .

Absolute (*rising*) 'Sdeath! You rascal! You have not trusted him!

Fag. O, *no*, sir—no—no—not a syllable, upon my veracity! He was, indeed, a little inquisitive; but I was sly, sir—devilish sly! My master (said I), honest Thomas (you know, sir, one says *honest* to one's inferiors), is come to Bath to *recruit*—yes, sir, I said to *recruit*—and whether for men, money, or constitution, you know, sir, is nothing to him, nor anyone else.

Absolute (*turning up stage to the fireplace, still trimming his nails*) Well, *recruit* will do—let it be so.

Fag. O, sir, recruit will do surprisingly—indeed, to give the thing an air, I told Thomas that your honour had already enlisted five disbanded chairmen, seven minority waiters, and thirteen billiard-markers.

Absolute (*turning*) You blockhead, never say more than is necessary.

Fag. I beg pardon, sir—I beg pardon—but, with submission, a lie is nothing unless one supports it. Sir, whenever I draw on

my invention for a good current lie, I always forge indorsements
as well as the bill.

ABSOLUTE. Well, take care you don't hurt your credit by offer-
ing too much security. Is Mr Faulkland returned?

FAG. He is above, sir, changing his dress.

ABSOLUTE. Can you tell whether he has been informed of Sir
Anthony and Miss Melville's arrival?

FAG. I fancy not, sir; he has seen no-one since he came in
but his gentleman, who was with him at Bristol. I think, sir, I
hear Mr Faulkland coming down . . .

ABSOLUTE. Go, tell him I am here.

FAG. Yes, sir. (*He goes to the door* L, *then turns*) I beg pardon, sir,
but should Sir Anthony call, you will do me the favour to remember that we are *recruiting*, if you please.

ABSOLUTE. Well, well.

FAG. And, in tenderness to my character, if your honour
could bring in the chairmen and waiters, I would esteem it as
an obligation; for though I never scruple a lie to serve my master,
yet it hurts one's conscience to be found out.

(FAG *exits* L)

ABSOLUTE (*coming down* C) Now for my whimsical friend—if he
does not know that his mistress is here, I'll tease him a little before
I tell him.

(FAULKLAND *enters* L, *introduced by* FAG. *He crosses to Absolute.*
FAG *exits*)

Faulkland, you're welcome to Bath again; you are punctual
in your return.

FAULKLAND. Yes; I had nothing to detain me, when I had
finished the business I went on.

(*They move to the chairs up stage.* ABSOLUTE *sits* R, FAULKLAND
sits L)

Well, what news, since I left you? How stand matters between
you and Lydia?

ABSOLUTE. Faith, much as they were; I have not seen her since
our quarrel; however, I expect to be recalled every hour.

FAULKLAND. Why don't you persuade her to go off with you
at once?

ABSOLUTE. What, and lose two-thirds of her fortune? You forget that, my friend. No, no, I could have brought her to that
long ago.

FAULKLAND. Nay, then, you trifle too long—if you are sure of
her, propose to the aunt, *in your own character*, and write to Sir
Anthony for his consent.

ABSOLUTE. Softly, softly; for though I am convinced my little
Lydia would elope with me as Ensign Beverley, yet I am by

no means certain that she would take me with the impediment of our friends' consent, a regular humdrum wedding, and the reversion of a good fortune on my side; no, no; I must prepare her gradually for the discovery, and make myself necessary to her, before I risk it. Well, but, Faulkland, you'll dine with us today at the hotel?

FAULKLAND. Indeed, I cannot; I am not in spirits to be of such a party.

ABSOLUTE. By heavens! I shall forswear your company. You are the most teasing, captious, incorrigible lover! Do love like a man.

FAULKLAND. I own I am unfit for company.

ABSOLUTE. Am not *I* a lover; ay, and a romantic one too? Yet do I carry everywhere with me such a confounded farrago of doubts, fears, hopes, wishes, and all the flimsy furniture of a country miss's brain?

FAULKLAND. Ah! Jack, your heart and soul are not, like mine, fixed immutably on one only object. You throw for a large stake, but losing, you could stake and throw again: but I have set my sum of happiness on this cast, and not to succeed were to be stript of all.

ABSOLUTE. But, for Heaven's sake! What grounds for apprehension can your whimsical brain conjure up at present?

FAULKLAND (*sitting forward; his hands on the arms of the chair*) What grounds for apprehension, did you say? Heavens! (*rising*) are there not a thousand! (*Moving a little down* L) I fear for her spirits—her health—her life. [My absence may fret her; her anxiety for my return, her fears for me may oppress her gentle temper. And for her health, does not every hour bring me cause to be alarmed? If it rains, some shower may even then have chilled her delicate frame! If the wind be keen, some rude blast may have affected her! The heat of noon, the dews of the evening may endanger the life of her, for whom only I value mine.] (*Going to the fireplace*) O Jack! when delicate and feeling souls are separated, there is not a feature in the sky, not a movement of the elements, not an aspiration of the breeze, but hints some cause for a lover's apprehension!

ABSOLUTE (*rising and bringing him down* C) Ay, but we may choose whether we will take the hint or not. So, then, Faulkland, if you were convinced that Julia were well and in spirits, you would be entirely content?

FAULKLAND. I should be happy beyond measure—I am anxious only for that.

ABSOLUTE. Then to cure your anxiety at once—Miss Melville is in perfect health, and is at this moment in Bath.

FAULKLAND. Nay, Jack—don't trifle with me.

ABSOLUTE. She is arrived here with my father within this hour

FAULKLAND. Can you be serious?

ABSOLUTE. I thought you knew Sir Anthony better than to be surprised at a sudden whim of this kind. Seriously, then, it is as I tell you—upon my honour.

FAULKLAND. My dear friend! (*Going into the doorway* L) Hollo, Du Peigne! My hat. (*Returning*) My dear Jack—now nothing on earth can give me a moment's uneasiness.

(FAG *enters* R)

FAG. Sir, Mr Acres, just arrived, is below.

ABSOLUTE. Stay, Faulkland; this Acres lives within a mile of Sir Anthony, and he shall tell you how your mistress has been ever since you left her. (*Moving* C) Fag, show the gentleman up.

(FAG *exits* R)

FAULKLAND. What, is he much acquainted in the family?

ABSOLUTE. O, very intimate: [I insist on your not going: besides, his character will divert you.

FAULKLAND. Well, I should like to ask him a few questions.]

ABSOLUTE. He is likewise a rival of mine—that is, of my *other self's*, for he does not think his friend Captain Absolute ever saw the lady in question; and it is ridiculous enough to hear him complain to me of *one Beverley*, a concealed skulking rival, who . . .

FAULKLAND. Hush! He's here.

(ACRES *enters* R. ABSOLUTE *moves to him, and they meet* RC *and shake hands heartily*)

ACRES. Ha! my dear friend, noble captain, and honest Jack, how do'st thou? Just arrived, faith, as you see. Sir, your humble servant. Warm work on the roads, Jack! Odds whips and wheels! I've travelled like a comet, with a tail of dust all the way as long as the Mall.

ABSOLUTE. Ah! Bob, you are indeed an eccentric planet, but we know your attraction hither. Give me leave to introduce Mr Faulkland to you; Mr Faulkland, Mr Acres. (*He goes behind the chair* RC *and leans over the back of it*)

ACRES (*going to Faulkland, and shaking hands*) Sir, I am most heartily glad to see you: sir, I solicit your connections. Hey, Jack—what, this is Mr Faulkland, who . . .

ABSOLUTE. Ay, Bob, Miss Melville's Mr Faulkland.

ACRES. Od'so! She and your father can be but just arrived before me. I suppose you have seen them. Ah! Mr Faulkland, you are indeed a happy man.

FAULKLAND. I have not seen Miss Melville yet, sir; I hope she enjoyed full health and spirits in Devonshire?

ACRES. Never knew her better in my life, sir, never better. Odds blushes and blooms! She has been as healthy as the German Spa.

FAULKLAND. Indeed! I did hear that she had been a little indisposed-

ACRES. False, false, sir—only said to vex you: quite the reverse, I assure you. (*He turns up* C, *and takes a good look round*)

FAULKLAND (*moving to the chair* RC) There, Jack, you see she has the advantage of me; I had almost fretted myself ill.

ABSOLUTE. Now you are angry with your mistress for not having been sick?

FAULKLAND. No, no, you misunderstand me: yet surely a little trifling indisposition is not an unnatural consequence of absence from those we love. Now confess—isn't there something unkind in this violent, robust, unfeeling health?

ABSOLUTE. O, it is very unkind of her to be well in your absence, to be sure!

ACRES (*turning*) Good apartments, Jack.

FAULKLAND (*moving to Acres*) Well, sir, but you was saying that Miss Melville has been so *exceedingly* well—what, then, she has been merry and gay, I suppose? Always in spirits—hey?

ACRES. Merry, odds crickets! She has been the belle and spirit of the company wherever she has been—so lively and entertaining! So full of wit and humour!

FAULKLAND. There, Jack, there. Oh, by my soul! There is an innate levity in woman that nothing can overcome. What! happy, and I away!

ABSOLUTE (*coming round to the front of the chair and sitting on it*) Have done: how foolish this is! Just now you were only apprehensive for your mistress's *spirits*.

FAULKLAND. Why, Jack, have I been the joy and spirit of the company?

ABSOLUTE. No, indeed, you have not.

FAULKLAND. Have I been lively and entertaining?

ABSOLUTE. O, upon my word, I acquit you.

FAULKLAND. Have I been full of wit and humour?

ABSOLUTE. No, faith; to do you justice, you have been confoundedly stupid indeed.

(FAULKLAND *moves abruptly across to the chair at the table* L)

ACRES. What's the matter with the gentleman!

ABSOLUTE. He is only expressing his great satisfaction of hearing that Julia has been so well and happy—that's all. Hey, Faulkland?

FAULKLAND (*coming down* L) O! I am rejoiced to hear it. Yes, yes, she has a *happy* disposition!

ACRES. That she has indeed. Then she is so accomplished—so sweet a voice—so expert at her harpsichord—such a mistress of flat and sharp, squallante, rumblante, and quiverante! There was this time month—odds minims and crotchets! How did she chirrup at Mrs Piano's concert!

FAULKLAND (*turning sharply*) There again, what say you to this?

(*Coming* LC) You see she has been all mirth and song—not a thought of me!

ABSOLUTE. Pho man! Is not music the food of love?

FAULKLAND. Well, well, it may be so. Pray, Mr —— what's his d——d name? Do you remember what songs Miss Melville sung?

ACRES. Not I, indeed.

ABSOLUTE. Stay, now, they were some pretty melancholy purling-stream airs, I warrant; perhaps you may recollect; did she sing, *When absent from my soul's delight?*

ACRES. No, that wa'n't it.

ABSOLUTE. Or, *Go, gentle gales!* (*He sings*) "Go, gentle gales!"

ACRES. Oh, no! Nothing like it. (*Coming down* C) Odds! Now I recollect one of them—*My heart's my own, my will is free.*

FAULKLAND (*moving to the chair by the table* L, *sitting, and beating the table in emphasis*) Fool! Fool that I am! To fix all my happiness on such a trifler! 'Sdeath! To make herself the pipe and ballad-monger of a circle! To soothe her light heart with catches and glees! (*Sweeping round in the chair*) What can you say to this, sir?

ABSOLUTE. Why, that I should be glad to hear my mistress had been so *merry*, sir.

FAULKLAND. Nay, nay, nay—I'm not sorry that she has been happy—no, no, I am glad of that. [I would not have had her sad or sick—yet surely a sympathetic heart would have shown itself even in the choice of a song—she might have been temperately healthy, and somehow, plaintively gay]; but she has been dancing too, I doubt not!

ACRES (*moving to Absolute*) What does the gentleman say about dancing?

ABSOLUTE. He says the lady we speak of dances as well as she sings.

ACRES. Ay, truly, does she—(*going towards Faulkland*) there was at our last race ball . . .

FAULKLAND (*rising*) Hell and the devil! (*Crossing to Absolute*) There! There—I told you so! I told you so! Oh! She thrives in my absence! Dancing! But her whole feelings have been in opposition with mine; I have been anxious, silent, pensive, sedentary—my days have been hours of care, my nights of watchfulness. She has been all health! Spirit! Laugh! Song! Dance! (*Moving down* R) Damned, damned levity!

ABSOLUTE (*rising and going to Faulkland*) For Heaven's sake, Faulkland, don't expose yourself so! Suppose she had danced, what then? Does not the ceremony of society often oblige . . .

FAULKLAND. Well well, I'll contain myself—perhaps as you say —for form sake. What, Mr Acres, you were praising Miss Melville's manner of dancing a *minuet*—hey?

ACRES. O, I dare insure her for that—(*coming to* C) but what I was going to speak of was her country dancing. Odds swimmings! She has such an air with her.

FAULKLAND. Now disappointment on her! (*Turning to Absolute*) Defend this, Absolute; why don't you defend this? (*Going up to* R *of the chair* RC) Country dances! Jigs and reels! (*Turning to Absolute*) Am I to blame now? A minuet I could have forgiven—I should not have minded that—I say I should not have regarded a minuet—but *country-dances!* Zounds! [Had she made one in a *cotillon*—I believe I could have forgiven even that—but to be monkey-led for a night! To run the gauntlet through a string of amorous palming puppies! To show paces like a managed filly!] (*Going up stage and turning to Absolute*) Oh, Jack, there never can be but *one* man in the world whom a truly modest and delicate woman ought to pair with in a *country-dance*; and, even then, the rest of the couples should be her great-uncles and aunts!

ABSOLUTE. Ay, to be sure! Grandfathers and grandmothers!

FAULKLAND (*coming down to the chair* RC) If there be but one vicious mind in the set, 'twill spread like a contagion—the action of their pulse beats to the lascivious movement of the jig—their quivering, warm-breathed sighs impregnate the very air—the atmosphere becomes electrical to love, and each amorous spark darts through every link of the chain! (*Crossing to the door* L) I must leave you—I own I am somewhat flurried—and that confounded looby has perceived it.

ABSOLUTE. Nay, but stay, Faulkland, and thank Mr Acres for his good news.

FAULKLAND (*turning*) D——n his news!

(FAULKLAND *exits* L)

ABSOLUTE. Ha! ha! ha! Poor Faulkland five minutes since— "nothing on earth could give him a moment's uneasiness"!

ACRES (*moving* C) The gentleman wa'n't angry at my praising his mistress, was he?

ABSOLUTE. A little jealous, I believe, Bob.

ACRES. You don't say so? Ha! ha! Jealous of me—that's a good joke.

ABSOLUTE. There's nothing strange in that, Bob; let me tell you, that sprightly grace and insinuating manner of yours will do some mischief among the girls here.

ACRES (*going to Absolute*) Ah! you joke—ha! ha! Mischief—ha! ha! But you know I am not my own property; my dear Lydia has forestalled me. She could never abide me in the country, because I used to dress so badly—but odds frogs and tambours! I shan't take matters so here, now ancient madam has no voice in it; I'll make my old clothes know who's master. I shall straightway cashier the hunting-frock, and render my leather breeches incapable. My hair has been in training some time.

ABSOLUTE. Indeed!

ACRES. Ay—and tho' the side curls are a little restive, my hind-part takes it very kindly.

ABSOLUTE. Oh, you'll polish, I doubt not.

ACRES. Absolutely I propose so—then if I can find out this Ensign Beverley, odds triggers and flints! I'll make him know the difference o't.

ABSOLUTE. Spoke like a man! But pray, Bob, I observe you have got an odd kind of a new method of swearing . . .

ACRES. Ha! ha! You've taken notice of it—'tis genteel, *isn't* it! I didn't invent it myself though; but a commander in our militia, a great scholar, I assure you, says that there is no meaning in the common oaths, and that nothing but their antiquity makes them respectable—because, he says, the ancients would never stick to an oath or two, but would say, by Jove! or by Bacchus! or by Mars! or by Venus! or by Pallas! according to the sentiment— so that to swear with propriety, says my little major, "the oath should be an echo to the sense"; and this we call the *oath referential*, or *sentimental swearing*. Ha! ha! ha! 'Tis genteel, isn't it?

ABSOLUTE. Very genteel, and very new, indeed! And I dare say will supplant all other figures of imprecation.

ACRES. Ay, ay, the best terms will grow obsolete. Damns have had their day.

(FAG *enters* R)

FAG. Sir, there is a gentleman below desires to see you. Shall I show him into the parlour?

ABSOLUTE. Ay—you may.

ACRES. Well, I must be gone . . .

ABSOLUTE (*rising and moving to Fag*) Stay; who is it, Fag?

FAG. Your father, sir.

ABSOLUTE. You puppy, why didn't you show him up directly?

(FAG *exits* R)

ACRES (*crossing Absolute to* R) You have business with Sir Anthony. I expect a message from Mrs Malaprop at my lodgings. I have sent also to my dear friend Sir Lucius O'Trigger. Adieu, Jack; we must meet at night, when you shall give me a dozen bumpers to little Lydia.

ABSOLUTE. That I will with all my heart.

(ACRES *exits* R)

(*Moving to* C) Now for a parental lecture—I hope he has heard nothing of the business that has brought me here—I wish the gout had held him fast in Devonshire, with all my soul!

(SIR ANTHONY ABSOLUTE *enters* R)

Sir, I am delighted to see you here; and looking so well! Your sudden arrival at Bath made me apprehensive for your health.

SIR ANTHONY (*sitting* RC) Very apprehensive, I dare say, Jack. What, you are recruiting here, hey?

ABSOLUTE. Yes, sir, I am on duty.

SIR ANTHONY. Well, Jack, I am glad to see you, though I did not expect it, for I was going to write to you on a little matter of business. Jack, I have been considering that I grow old and infirm, and shall probably not trouble you long.

ABSOLUTE. Pardon me, sir, I never saw you look more strong and hearty; and I pray frequently that you may continue so.

SIR ANTHONY. I hope your prayers may be heard, with all my heart. Well then, Jack, I have been considering that I am so strong and hearty I may continue to plague you a long time. Now, Jack, I am sensible that the income of your commission, and what I have hitherto allowed you, is but a small pittance for a lad of your spirit.

ABSOLUTE. Sir, you are very good.

SIR ANTHONY. And it is my wish, while yet I live, to have my boy make some figure in the world. I have resolved, therefore, to fix you at once in a noble independence.

ABSOLUTE. Sir, your kindness overpowers me—[such generosity makes the gratitude of reason more lively than the sensations even of filial affection.

SIR ANTHONY. I am glad you are so sensible of my attention —and you shall be master of a large estate in a few weeks.]

ABSOLUTE (*turning up to the chair* L *of the fireplace*) Let my future life, sir, speak my gratitude; [I cannot express the sense I have of your munificence] (*Turning to Sir Anthony*) Yet, sir, I presume you would not wish me to quit the army?

SIR ANTHONY. Oh, that shall be as your wife chooses.

ABSOLUTE. My wife, sir!

SIR ANTHONY. Ay, ay, settle that between you—settle that between you.

ABSOLUTE (*coming down* C) A *wife*, sir, did you say?

SIR ANTHONY. Ay, a wife. Why, did I not mention her before?

ABSOLUTE. Not a word of her, sir.

SIR ANTHONY. Odd so! I mustn't forget *her* though. Yes, Jack, the independence I was talking of is by a marriage—the fortune is saddled with a wife—but I suppose that makes no difference.

ABSOLUTE. Sir! sir! You amaze me!

SIR ANTHONY. Why, what the devil's the matter with the fool? Just now you were all gratitude and duty.

ABSOLUTE. I was, sir. You talked to me of independence and a fortune, but not a word of a wife.

SIR ANTHONY. Why—what difference does that make? Odds life, sir! If you have the estate, you must take it with the livestock on it, as it stands.

ABSOLUTE. If my happiness is to be the price, I must beg leave to decline the purchase. Pray, sir, who is the lady?

SIR ANTHONY. What's that to you, sir? Come, give me your promise to love, and to marry her directly.

ABSOLUTE. Sure, sir, this is not very reasonable, to summon my affections for a lady I know nothing of!

SIR ANTHONY. I am sure, sir, 'tis more unreasonable in you to *object* to a lady you know nothing of.

ABSOLUTE. Then, sir, I must tell you plainly that my inclinations are fixed on another—my heart is engaged to an angel.

SIR ANTHONY. Then pray let it send an excuse. It is very sorry but *business* prevents its waiting on her.

ABSOLUTE. But my vows are pledged to her.

SIR ANTHONY. Let her foreclose, Jack! Let her foreclose; they are not worth redeeming; besides, you have the angel's vows in exchange, I suppose; so there can be no loss there.

ABSOLUTE (*moving to* C) You must excuse me, sir, if I tell you, once for all, that in this point I cannot obey you.

SIR ANTHONY. Hark'ee, Jack; I have heard you for some time with patience—I have been cool—quite cool; but take care—you know I am compliance itself—when I am not thwarted; no-one more easily led—when I have my own way; but don't put me in a frenzy.

ABSOLUTE. Sir, I must repeat it—in this I cannot obey you.

SIR ANTHONY (*rising*) Now d——n me! If ever I call you Jack again while I live!

ABSOLUTE. Nay, sir, but hear me.

SIR ANTHONY. Sir, I won't hear a word—not a word! Not one word! (*With a step towards Absolute*) So give me your promise by a nod—and I'll tell you what, Jack—I mean, you dog—if you don't, by . . .

ABSOLUTE. What, sir, promise to link myself to some mass of ugliness! To . . .

SIR ANTHONY. Zounds! Sirrah! The lady shall be as ugly as I choose: she shall have a hump on each shoulder; she shall be as crooked as the Crescent; her one eye shall roll like the bull's in Cox's Museum; she shall have a skin like a mummy, and the beard of a Jew. She shall be all this, sirrah! Yet I will make you ogle her all day, and sit up all night to write sonnets on her beauty.

ABSOLUTE (*turns away a few steps down* L) This is reason and. moderation indeed!

SIR ANTHONY. None of your sneering, puppy! No grinning, jackanapes!

ABSOLUTE. Indeed, sir, I never was in a worse humour for mirth in my life.

SIR ANTHONY. 'Tis false, sir, I know you are laughing in your sleeve; I know you'll grin when I am gone, sirrah!

ABSOLUTE. Sir, I hope I know my duty better.

SIR ANTHONY. None of your passion, sir! None of your violence, if you please! It won't do with me, I promise you.

ABSOLUTE. Indeed, sir, I never was cooler in my life.

SIR ANTHONY. 'Tis a confounded lie! I know you are in a passion in your heart; I know you are, you hypocritical young dog! But it won't do.

ABSOLUTE (*turning to Sir Anthony*) Nay, sir, upon my word . . .

SIR ANTHONY. So you will fly out! Can't you be cool like me? What the devil good can *passion* do? *Passion* is of no service, you impudent, insolent, overbearing reprobate! There, you sneer again! Don't provoke me! But you rely upon the mildness of my temper—you do, you dog! You play upon the meekness of my disposition. Yet take care—the patience of a saint may be overcome at last! But mark! I give you six hours and a half to consider of this: if you then agree, without any condition, to do everything on earth that I choose, why—confound you!—I may in time forgive you. If not, zounds! Don't enter the same hemisphere with me! Don't dare to breathe the same air, or use the same light with me; but get an atmosphere and a sun of your own! I'll strip you of your commission; I'll lodge a five-and-threepence in the hands of trustees, and you shall live on the interest. I'll disown you, I'll disinherit you, I'll unget you! (*He moves to the door and turns*) And d——n me if ever I call you Jack again!

(SIR ANTHONY *exits* R)

ABSOLUTE. Mild, gentle, considerate father—I kiss your hands! What a tender method of giving his opinion in these matters Sir Anthony has! I dare not trust him with the truth. I wonder what old wealthy hag it is that he wants to bestow on me! Yet he married himself for love! And was in his youth a bold intriguer and a gay companion!

(FAG *enters* R)

FAG. Assuredly, sir, your father is wrath to a degree: he comes downstairs eight or ten steps at a time—muttering, growling, and thumping the banisters all the way: I and the cook's dog stand bowing at the door. He gives me a stroke on the head with his cane; bids me carry that to my master; then kicking the poor turnspit into the area, d——ns us all for a puppy triumvirate! Upon my credit, sir, were I in your place, and found my father such very bad company, I should certainly drop his acquaintance.

ABSOLUTE. Cease your impertinence, sir, at present. Did you come in for nothing more? Stand out of the way!

(ABSOLUTE *pushes Fag aside and exits* R)

FAG. Soh! Sir Anthony trims my master: he is afraid to reply to his father—then he vents his splee on poor Fag! When one is vexed by one person, to revenge one's self on another, who happens to come in the way, is the vilest injustice! Ah! it shows the worst temper—the basest . . .

(*An* ERRAND BOY *enters* R)

Boy. Mr Fag! Mr Fag! Your master calls you.

Fag. Well, you little dirty puppy, you need not bawl so! The meanest dispostion! The . . .

Boy. Quick, quick, Mr Fag!

Fag. Quick, quick, you impudent jackanapes! Am I to be commanded by you, too? You little impertinent, insolent, kitchen-bred . . .

(Fag *exits kicking and beating the* Errand Boy)

Scene 2

Scene—*The North Parade.*

Lucy *enters* l, *and moves* lc.

Lucy. So—I shall have another rival to add to my mistress's list—Captain Absolute. However, I shall not enter his name till my purse has received notice in form. Poor Acres is dismissed! Well, I have done him a last friendly office, in letting him know that Beverley was here before him. Sir Lucius is generally more punctual, when he expects to hear from his *dear Dalia,* as he calls her: I wonder he's not here! I have a little scruple of conscience from this deceit; though I should not be paid so well, if my hero knew that *Delia* was near fifty, and her own mistress.

(Sir Lucius O'Trigger *enters* r, *and crosses to Lucy*)

Sir Lucius. Hah! My little ambassadress—upon my conscience, I have been looking for you; I have been on the South Parade this half-hour.

Lucy (*simply*) Oh, Gemini! And I have been waiting for your worship here on the North.

Sir Lucius. Faith! May be that was the reason we did not meet; and it is very comical, too, how you could go out and I not see you—for I was only taking a nap at the Parade Coffee-house, and I chose the *window* on purpose that I might not miss you.

Lucy. My stars! Now I'd wager a sixpence I went by while you were asleep.

Sir Lucius. Sure enough it must have been so. And I never dreamt it was so late till I waked. Well, but, my little girl, have you got nothing for me?

Lucy. Yes, but I have—I've got a letter for you in my pocket.

Sir Lucius. Oh faith! I guessed you weren't come empty-handed. Well—let me see what the dear creature says.

Lucy. There, Sir Lucius. (*She gives him a letter*)

Sir Lucius (*reading it*) "Sir—there is often a sudden incentive impulse in love, that has a greater induction than years of domestic combination: such was the commotion I felt at the first superfluous view of Sir Lucius O'Trigger." Very pretty, upon my word. "Female punctuation forbids me to say more, yet let me add, that it will give me joy infallible to find Sir Lucius worthy the last criterion of my affections. Delia." Upon my conscience! Lucy, your lady is a great mistress of language. Faith, she's quite a queen of the dictionary—for the devil a word dare refuse coming at her call—though one would think it was quite out of hearing.

Lucy. Ay, sir, a lady of her experience . . .

Sir Lucius. Experience! What, at seventeen!

Lucy. Oh, true, sir—but then she reads so. My stars! How she will read offhand!

Sir Lucius. Faith, she must be very deep read to write this way—though she is rather an arbitrary writer too—for here are a great many poor words pressed into the service of this note, that would get their *habeas corpus* from any court in Christendom.

Lucy. Ah! Sir Lucius, if you were to hear how she talks of you!

Sir Lucius. Oh, tell her I'll make her the best husband in the world, and Lady O'Trigger into the bargain! But we must get the old gentlewoman's consent—and do everything fairly.

Lucy. Nay, Sir Lucius, I thought you wa'n't rich enough to be so nice.

Sir Lucius. Upon my word, young woman, you have hit it: I am so poor, that I can't afford to do a dirty action. If I did not want money, I'd steal your mistress and her fortune with a great deal of pleasure. However, my pretty girl, (*giving her money*), here's a little something to buy you a ribbon; and meet me in the evening, and I'll give you an answer to this. So, hussy, take a kiss beforehand to put you in mind. (*He kisses her*)

Lucy. Oh Lud! Sir Lucius—I never seed such a gemman! My lady won't like you if you're so impudent.

Sir Lucius. Faith she will, Lucy! That same. Who! What's the name of it?—*Modesty*—is a quality in a lover more praised by the woman than liked; so if your mistress asks you whether Sir Lucius ever gave you a kiss—tell her fifty, my dear.

Lucy. What, would you have me tell her a lie?

Sir Lucius. Ah, then, you baggage! I'll make it a truth presently.

Lucy. For shame now! Here is someone coming.

Sir Lucius. Oh faith, I'll get your conscience!

(Sir Lucius *sees someone coming from off* L, *and exits* R, *humming a tune.*

Fag *enters* L)

Fag. So, ma'am! I humbly beg pardon.

Lucy. Oh Lud! Now, Mr Fag, you flurry one so.

Fag. Come, come, Lucy, here's no-one by—so a little less simplicity, with a grain or two more sincerity, if you please. You play false with us, madam. I saw you give the baronet a letter. My master shall know this—and if he don't call him out, I will. (*He crosses to* RC)

Lucy. Ha! Ha! Ha! You gentlemen's gentlemen are so hasty. That letter was from Mrs Malaprop, simpleton. She is taken with Sir Lucius's address.

Fag. How! What tastes some people have! Why, I suppose I have walked by her window an hundred times. But what says our young lady? Any message to my master?

Lucy. Sad news, Mr Fag. A worse rival than Acres! Sir Anthony Absolute has proposed his son.

Fag. What, Captain Absolute?

Lucy. Even so—I overheard it all.

Fag. Ha! Ha! Ha! Very good, faith. Good-bye, Lucy; I must be away with the news.

Lucy. Well, you may laugh—but it is true, I assure you. (*Going*) But, Mr Fag, tell your master not to be cast down by this.

Fag. Oh, he'll be so disconsolate!

Lucy. And charge him not to think of quarrelling with young Absolute.

Fag. Never fear! Never fear!

Lucy. Be sure—bid him to keep up his spirits.

Fag. We will—we will.

(Fag *exits* R. Lucy *exits* L)

ACT III

Scene i

SCENE—*The North Parade.*

When the CURTAIN *rises,* ABSOLUTE *enters* L.

ABSOLUTE. 'Tis just as Fag told me, indeed. Whimsical enough, faith! My father wants to *force* me to marry the very girl I am plotting to run away with! He must not know of my connexion with her yet awhile. He has too summary a method of proceeding in these matters. However, I'll read my recantation instantly. My conversion is something *sudden*, indeed—but I can assure him it is very *sincere*. So, so, here he comes. He looks plaguy gruff. (*He turns away up* L, *going up stage*)

(SIR ANTHONY *enters* R, *and moves to* RC)

SIR ANTHONY. No—I'll die sooner than forgive him. *Die*, did I say? I'll live these fifty years to plague him. At our last meeting, his impudence had almost put me out of temper. An obstinate, passionate, self-willed boy! Who can he take after? This is my return for getting him before all his brothers and sisters! For putting him, at twelve years old, into a marching regiment, and allowing him fifty pounds a year, besides his pay, ever since! But I have done with him; he's anybody's son for me. I will never see him more, never—never—never. (*He starts to move* L)

ABSOLUTE (*coming forward; aside*) Now for a penitential face. (*He is now in Sir Anthony's path*)

SIR ANTHONY. Fellow, get out of my way!

ABSOLUTE. Sir, you see a penitent before you.

SIR ANTHONY. I see an impudent scoundrel before me.

ABSOLUTE. A sincere penitent. I am come, sir, to acknowledge my error, and to submit entirely to your will.

SIR ANTHONY (*moving to him*) What's that?

ABSOLUTE. I have been revolving, and reflecting, and considering on your past goodness, and kindness, and condescension to me.

SIR ANTHONY. Well, sir?

ABSOLUTE. I have been likewise weighing and balancing what you were pleased to mention concerning duty, and obedience, and authority.

SIR ANTHONY. Well, puppy?

ABSOLUTE. Why then, sir, the result of my reflections is—a resolution to sacrifice every inclination of my own to your satisfaction.

SIR ANTHONY. Why, now you talk sense—absolute sense—I never heard anything more sensible in my life. Confound you! You shall be Jack again.

ABSOLUTE. I am happy in the appellation.

SIR ANTHONY (*putting a hand on Absolute's shoulder*) Why then, Jack, my dear Jack, I will now inform you who the lady really is. Nothing but passion and violence, you silly fellow, prevented my telling you at first. Prepare, Jack, for wonder and rapture— prepare. What think you of Miss Lydia Languish?

ABSOLUTE. Languish? What, the Languishes of Worcestershire?

SIR ANTHONY. Worcestershire! No. Did you never meet Mrs Malaprop and her niece, Miss Languish, who came into our country just before you were last ordered to your regiment?

ABSOLUTE. Malaprop! Languish! I don't remember ever to have heard the names before. Yet, stay—I think I do recollect something. *Languish! Languish!* She squints, don't she? A little red-haired girl?

SIR ANTHONY. Squints! A red-haired girl! Zounds, no!

ABSOLUTE. Then I must have forgot; it can't be the same person.

SIR ANTHONY. Jack! Jack! What think you of blooming, love-breathing seventeen?

ABSOLUTE. As to that, sir, I am quite indifferent. If I can please you in the matter, 'tis all I desire.

SIR ANTHONY. Nay, but, Jack, such eyes! Such eyes! So innocently wild! So bashfully irresolute! Not a glance but speaks and kindles some thought of love! Then, Jack, her cheeks! Her cheeks, Jack! So deeply blushing at the insinuations of her tell-tale eyes! Then, Jack, her lips! Oh Jack, lips smiling at their own discretion; and if not smiling, more sweetly pouting; more lovely in sullenness!

ABSOLUTE (*aside*) That's she, indeed! Well done, old gentleman.

SIR ANTHONY. Then, Jack, her neck! Oh, Jack, Jack!

ABSOLUTE. And which is to be mine, sir, the niece, or the aunt?

SIR ANTHONY. Why, you unfeeling, insensible puppy, I despise you! When I was of your age, such a description would have made me fly like a rocket! The *aunt*, indeed! Odds life! When I ran away with your mother, I would not have touched anything old or ugly to gain an empire.

ABSOLUTE. Not to please your father, sir?

SIR ANTHONY. To please my father! Zounds! Not to please . . . Oh, my father—odd so! Yes—yes; if my father indeed had desired—that's quite another matter. Though he wa'n't the indulgent father that I am, Jack.

ABSOLUTE. I dare say not, sir.

SIR ANTHONY. But, Jack, you are not sorry to find your mistress is so beautiful?

ABSOLUTE. Sir, I repeat it—if I please you in this affair, 'tis all I desire. Not that I think a woman the worse for being handsome; but, sir, if you please to recollect, you before hinted something about a hump or two, one eye, and a few more graces of that kind —now, without being very nice, I own I should rather choose a wife of mine to have the usual number of limbs, and a limited quantity of back: and though *one* eye may be very agreeable, yet as the prejudice has always run in favour of *two*, I would not wish to affect a singularity in that article.

SIR ANTHONY. What a phlegmatic sot it is! Why, sirrah, you're an anchorite—a vile, insensible stock! You a soldier! You're a walking block, fit only to dust the company's regimentals on! (*Crossing to* RC) Odds life! I have a great mind to marry the girl myself.

ABSOLUTE. I am entirely at your disposal, sir: if you should think of addressing Miss Languish yourself, I suppose you would have me marry the *aunt*; or if you should change your mind, and take the old lady—'tis the same to me—I'll marry the *niece*.

SIR ANTHONY (*moving to Absolute*) Upon my word, Jack, thou'rt either a very great hypocrite, or . . . But, come, I know your indifference on such a subject must be all a lie—I'm sure it must—come, now—d—n your demure face! Come, confess, Jack—you have been lying—ha'n't you? You have been playing the hypocrite, hey! I'll never forgive you, if you ha'n't been lying and playing the hypocrite.

ABSOLUTE. I'm sorry, sir, that the respect and duty which I bear to you should be so mistaken.

SIR ANTHONY. Hang your respect and duty! But come along with me. (*He crosses* L) I'll write a note to Mrs Malaprop, and you shall visit the lady directly. Her eyes shall be the Promethean torch to you—come along, I'll never forgive you, if you don't come back stark mad with rapture and impatience—if you don't, egad, I'll marry the girl myself!

(*Exeunt* L)

SCENE 2

SCENE—*Julia's dressing-room.*

FAULKLAND *enters* L *and moves* LC.

FAULKLAND. They told me Julia would return directly; I wonder she has not yet come! (*Moving behind the sofa*) How mean does this captious, unsatisfied temper of mine appear to my cooler judgement? Yet I know not that I indulge it in any other point: but on this one subject, and to this one subject, whom I think I love beyond my life, I am ever ungenerously fretful and madly capricious! I am conscious of it—yet I cannot correct myself!

[What tender honest joy sparkled in her eyes when we met! How delicate was the warmth of her expressions! (*Moving round* R *of the sofa and in front of it*) I was ashamed to appear less happy—(*He stops* C) though I had come resolved to wear a face of coolness and upbraiding. Sir Anthony's presence prevented my proposed expostulations: yet I must be satisfied that she has not been so *very* happy in my absence.]* She is coming! Yes! I know the nimbleness of her tread, when she thinks her impatient Faulkland counts the moments of her stay. (*He moves down* L)

(JULIA *enters* R, *and crosses to the sofa*)

JULIA. I had not hoped to see you again so soon.

FAULKLAND (*crossing to her*) Could I, Julia, be contented with my first welcome—restrained as we were by the presence of a third person?

(*They sit on the sofa*)

JULIA. Oh, Faulkland, when your kindness can make me thus happy, let me not think that I discovered something of coldness in your first salutation.

FAULKLAND. 'Twas but your fancy, Julia. I *was* rejoiced to see you—to see you in such health. Sure I had no cause for coldness?

JULIA. Nay, then, I see you have taken something ill. You must not conceal from me what it is.

FAULKLAND. Well, then—shall I own to you that my joy at hearing of your health and arrival here, by your neighbour Acres, was somewhat damped by his dwelling much on the high spirits you had enjoyed in Devonshire—on your mirth—your singing—dancing, and I know not what! For such is my temper, Julia, that I should regard every mirthful moment in your absence as a treason to constancy. The mutual tear that steals down the cheek of parting lovers is a compact, that no smile shall live there till they meet again.

JULIA. Must I never cease to tax my Faulkland with this teasing minute caprice? Can the idle reports of a silly boor weigh in your breast against my tried affection?

FAULKLAND. They have no weight with me, Julia: no, no—I am happy if you have been so—(*dropping on one knee*) yet only say, that you did not sing with *mirth*—say that you *thought* of Faulkland in the dance.

JULIA. I never can be happy in your absence. [If I wear a countenance of content, it is to show that my mind holds no doubt of my Faulkland's truth. If I seemed sad, it were to make malice triumph, and say, that I had fixed my heart on one, who left me to lament his roving, and my own credulity. Believe me,

---

* If this cut is made, he moves round in front of the sofa on the line "I am conscious of it . . ."

Faulkland, I mean not to upbraid you, when I say, that I have often dressed sorrow in smiles, lest my friends should guess whose unkindness had caused my tears.

FAULKLAND. You were ever all goodness to me. (*With his head on her knee*) Oh, I am a brute, when I but admit a doubt of your true constancy!]

JULIA. If ever without such cause from you, as I will not suppose possible, you find my affections veering but a point, may I become a proverbial scoff for levity and base ingratitude.

FAULKLAND (*rising; sharply*) Ah! Julia, that last word is grating to me. (*Moving away* L) I would I had no title to your *gratitude!* (*He turns towards Julia*) Search your heart, Julia; perhaps what you have mistaken for love, is but the warm effusion of a too thankful heart.

JULIA. [For what quality must I love you?

FAULKLAND. For no quality! To regard me for any quality of mind or understanding, were only to *esteem* me. And for person— I have often wished myself deformed, to be convinced that I owed no obligation *there* for any part of your affection.

JULIA. Where nature has bestowed a show of nice attention in the features of a man, he should laugh at it as misplaced. I have seen men, who in *this* vain article, perhaps, might rank above you; but my heart has never asked my eyes if it were so or not.

FAULKLAND. Now this is not well from *you*, Julia—I despise person in a man—yet if you loved me as I wish, though I were an Æthiop, you'd think none so fair.]

JULIA. I see you are determined to be unkind! The *contract* which my poor father bound us in gives you more than a lover's privilege.

FAULKLAND (*moving in to the sofa*) Again, Julia, you raise ideas that feed and justify my doubts. I would not have been more free —no—I am proud of my restraint. (*Leaning over the arm of the sofa*) Yet—yet—perhaps your high respect alone for this solemn compact has fettered your inclinations, which else had made a worthier choice. [How shall I be sure, had you remained unbound in thought and promise, that I should still have been the object of your persevering love?

JULIA. Then try me now.] Let us be free as strangers as to what is past: *my* heart will not feel more liberty!

FAULKLAND (*standing upright*) There now! So hasty, Julia! So anxious to be free? If your love for me were fixed and ardent, you would not loose your hold even though I wished it!

JULIA. Oh, you torture me to the heart! I cannot bear it. (*She hides her face in her hands*)

FAULKLAND (*sitting beside her, and taking her hand*) I do not mean to distress you. If I loved you less I should never give you an uneasy moment. But hear me. All my fretful doubts arise from this. Women are not used to weigh and separate the motives of their affections: the cold dictates of prudence, gratitude, or filial duty, may sometimes be mistaken for the pleadings of the heart. I would not boast—yet let me say, that I have neither age, person, nor character, to found dislike on; my fortune such as few ladies could be charged with *indiscretion* in the match.] Oh, Julias When *love* receives such countenance from *prudence*, nice mind! will be suspicious of its birth.

Julia (*rising*) I know not whither your insinuations would tend: but as they seem pressing to insult me, I will spare you the regret of having done so. (*She turns* R, *to the door*) I have given you no cause for this!

(Julia *exits* R *in tears*)

Faulkland (*rising*) In tears! Stay, Julia: (*going to the door* R) stay but for a moment. The door is fastened! Julia! My soul—but for one moment! I hear her sobbing! (*Moving* C) 'Sdeath! What a brute am I to use her thus! (*He stops suddenly; listening*) Yet stay! Ay—she is coming now: (*moving* LC) how little resolution there is in a woman! How a few soft words can turn them! No, faith, she is *not* coming either! (*Going up* C, *and appealing to the door*) Why, Julia—my love—say that you forgive me—come but to tell me that. Now this is being *too* resentful. (*He stops*) Stay! She is coming too—I thought she would—no *steadiness* in anything: her going away must have been a mere trick then—she sha'n't see that I was hurt by it. I'll affect indifference. (*He turns up stage* L, *humming a tune. Then he stops and looks over his shoulder towards the door* R, *listening. He turns sharply towards the door*) No—zounds! She's not coming! Nor don't intend it, I suppose. (*He moves impetuously to the upstage* L *corner of the sofa, and hits it for emphasis*) This is not *steadiness*, but *obstinacy!* (*With a sigh, as he moves slowly down* L) Yet I deserve it. (*He stops*) What, after so long an absence to quarrel with her tenderness! (*Moving* R *and back again to* LC) 'Twas barbarous and unmanly! I should be ashamed to see her now. (*Stopping*) I'll wait till her just resentment is abated—and when I distress her so again, may I lose her for ever, and be linked instead to some antique virago, whose gnawing passions and long-hoarded spleen shall make me curse my folly half the day and all the night.

(Faulkland *exits* L)

SCENE 3

Scene—*Mrs Malaprop's lodgings.*

Mrs Malaprop *and* Captain Absolute *enter from* L. *Mrs Malaprop has a letter in her hand. They cross to* C.

MRS MALAPROP. Your being Sir Anthony's son, Captain, would itself be a sufficient accommodation; but from the ingenuity of your appearance, I am convinced you deserve the character here given of you.

ABSOLUTE. Permit me to say, madam, that as I never yet have had the pleasure of seeing Miss Languish, my principal inducement in this affair at present is the honour of being allied to Mrs Malaprop, of whose intellectual accomplishments, elegant manners, and unaffected learning, no tongue is silent.

MRS MALAPROP. Sir, you do me infinite honour! I beg, Captain, you'll be seated.

(ABSOLUTE *brings the chair from* L *to* C *and then the other chair from up* LC *and sets it beside it.* MRS MALAPROP *curtsies,* ABSOLUTE *bows, and they sit* R *and* L *respectively*)

Ah! Few gentlemen, nowadays, know how to value the ineffectual qualities in a woman! Few think how a little knowledge becomes a gentlewoman! Men have no sense now but for the worthless flower of beauty!

ABSOLUTE. It is but too true, indeed, ma'am; yet I fear our ladies should share the blame—they think our admiration of *beauty* so great, that *knowledge* in *them* would be superfluous. Thus, like garden trees, they seldom show fruit till time has robbed them of the more specious blossom. Few, like Mrs Malaprop and the orange tree, are rich in both at once.

(*They both rise.* MRS MALAPROP *curtsies,* ABSOLUTE *bows*)

MRS MALAPROP. Sir, you overpower me with good breeding.

(*They both sit*)

(*Aside*) He is the very pineapple of politeness! You are not ignorant, Captain, that this giddy girl has somehow contrived to fix her affections on a beggarly, strolling, eavesdropping ensign, whom none of us have seen, and nobody knows anything of.

ABSOLUTE. Oh, I have heard the silly affair before. I'm not at all prejudiced against her on *that* account.

MRS MALAPROP. You are very good and very considerate, Captain. I am sure I have done everything in my power since I exploded the affair; long ago I laid my positive conjunctions on her, never to think on the fellow again. I have since laid Sir Anthony's preposition before her; but, I am sorry to say, she seems resolved to decline every particle that I enjoin her.

ABSOLUTE. It must be very distressing, indeed, ma'am.

MRS MALAPROP. Oh, it gives me the hydrostatics to such a degree! I thought she had persisted from corresponding with him; but, behold, this very day I have interceded another letter from the fellow; I believe I have it in my pocket.

ABSOLUTE (*aside*) Oh, the devil! My last note!

MRS MALAPROP. Ay, here it is.

ABSOLUTE (*aside*) Ay, my note, indeed! Oh, the little traitress Lucy.

MRS MALAPROP. There, perhaps you may know the writing. (*She gives him the letter*)

ABSOLUTE. I think I have seen the hand before—yes, I certainly must have seen this hand before . . .

MRS MALAPROP. Nay, but read it, Captain.

ABSOLUTE (*reading*) "My soul's idol, my adored Lydia!" Very tender indeed!

MRS MALAPROP. Tender! Ay, and profane too, o' my conscience.

ABSOLUTE (*reading*) "I am excessively alarmed at the intelligence you send me, the more so as my new rival——

MRS MALAPROP. That's *you*, sir.

ABSOLUTE (*reading*) —"has universally the character of being an accomplished gentleman and a man of honour." Well, that's handsome enough.

MRS MALAPROP. Oh, the fellow has some design in writing so.

ABSOLUTE. That he had, I'll answer for him, ma'am.

MRS MALAPROP. But go on, sir—you'll see presently.

ABSOLUTE (*reading*) "As for the old weather-beaten she-dragon who guards you." Who can he mean by that?

MRS MALAPROP. Me, sir! *Me!* He means *me!* There—what do you think now? But go on a little further.

ABSOLUTE. Impudent scoundrel! (*He reads*) —" it shall go hard but I will elude her vigilance, as I am told that the same ridiculous vanity, which makes her dress up her coarse features, and deck her dull chat with hard words which she don't understand . . ."

MRS MALAPROP. There, sir, an attack upon my language! What do you think of that? An aspersion upon my parts of speech! Was ever such a brute? Sure, if I reprehend anything in this world, it is the use of my oracular tongue, and a nice derangement of epitaphs!

ABSOLUTE. He deserves to be hanged and quartered! Let me see. (*He reads*) "Same ridiculous vanity——"

MRS MALAPROP. You need not read it again, sir.

ABSOLUTE. I beg pardon, ma'am. (*He reads*) "—does also lay her open to the grossest deceptions from flattery and pretended admiration"—an impudent coxcomb!—"so that I have a scheme to see you shortly with the old harridan's consent, and even to make her a go-between in our interview." Was ever such assurance!

MRS MALAPROP. Did you ever hear anything like it? He'll elude my vigilance, will he? Yes, yes! Ha! Ha! He's very likely to enter these doors. We'll try who can plot best!

ABSOLUTE. So we will, ma'am! So we will! Ha! Ha! Ha! A

conceited puppy! Ha! Ha! Ha! Well, but, Mrs Malaprop, as the girl seems so infatuated by this fellow, suppose you were to wink at her corresponding with him for a little time—let her even plot an elopement with him—then do you connive at her escape— while *I*, just in the nick, will have the fellow laid by the heels, and fairly contrive to carry her off in his stead.

MRS MALAPROP. I am delighted with the scheme; never was anything better perpetrated!

ABSOLUTE. But, pray, could not I see the lady for a few minutes now? I should like to try her temper a little.

MRS MALAPROP. Why, I don't know . . . I doubt she is not prepared for a visit of this kind. There is a decorum in these matters.

ABSOLUTE. O Lord! She won't mind me—only tell her Beverley . . .

MRS MALAPROP. Sir!

ABSOLUTE (*rising; aside*) Gently, good tongue.

MRS MALAPROP. What did you say of Beverley?

ABSOLUTE. Oh, I was going to propose that you should tell her, by way of jest, that it was Beverley who was below; she'd come down fast enough then. Ha! Ha! Ha!

MRS MALAPROP. 'Twould be a trick she well deserves; besides, you know the fellow tells her he'll get my consent to see her. Ha! Ha! Let him if he can, I say again. (*She rises, goes up* C *and calls off* R) Lydia, come down here! He'll make me a *go-between in their interviews!* Ha! Ha! Ha! Come down, I say, Lydia! (*Coming behind the chairs* C) I don't wonder at your laughing. Ha! Ha! Ha! His impudence is truly ridiculous.

ABSOLUTE. 'Tis very ridiculous, upon my soul, ma'am. Ha! Ha! Ha!

MRS MALAPROP. The little hussy won't hear. (*She goes up* C) Well, I'll go and tell her at once who it is—she shall know that Captain Absolute is come to wait on her. And I'll make her behave as becomes a young woman.

ABSOLUTE. As you please, ma'am.

MRS MALAPROP. For the present, Captain, your servant. Ah! You've not done laughing yet, I see.—*elude my vigilance!* Yes, yes! Ha! Ha! Ha!

(MRS MALAPROP *exits up* C *and goes off* R)

ABSOLUTE. Ha! Ha! Ha! One would think now that I might throw off all disguise at once, and seize my prize with security; but such is Lydia's caprice, that to undeceive were probably to lose her. I'll see whether she knows me. (*He crosses to the window* L *and looks out*)

(LYDIA *enters up* C *from* R. *She looks at Absolute, and then comes down* R, *to* R *of the chairs*)

LYDIA. What a scene am I now to go through! Surely nothing can be more dreadful than to be obliged to listen to the loathsome addresses of a stranger to one's heart. I have heard of girls persecuted as I am, who have appealed in behalf of their favoured lover to the generosity of his rival; suppose I were to try it—there stands the hated rival—an officer too!—But oh, unlike my Beverley! I wonder he don't begin—truly he seems a very negligent wooer!—Quite at his ease, upon my word!—I'll speak first—Mr Absolute.

ABSOLUTE. Ma'am. (*He turns round*)

(*There is a slight pause.* LYDIA *turns to him*)

LYDIA. Oh heavens! Beverley!

(*They cross towards each other, meeting* LC, *and take hands*)

ABSOLUTE. Hush! Hush, my life! Softly! Be not surprised!

LYDIA. I am so astonished! And so terrified! And so overjoyed! For Heaven's sake! How came you here?

ABSOLUTE (*leading her down* L) Briefly, I have deceived your aunt. I was informed that my new rival was to visit here this evening, and contriving to have him kept away, have passed myself on *her* for Captain Absolute.

LYDIA. Oh, charming! And she really takes you for young Absolute?

ABSOLUTE. Oh, she's convinced of it.

LYDIA. Ha! Ha! Ha! I can't forbear laughing to think how her sagacity is overreached!

ABSOLUTE. But we trifle with our precious moments—such another opportunity may not occur; then let me now conjure my kind, my condescending angel, to fix the time when I may rescue her from undeserved persecution, and with a licensed warmth plead for my reward.

LYDIA. Will you then, Beverley, consent to forfeit that portion of my paltry wealth; that burden on the wings of love?

ABSOLUTE. Oh, come to me—rich only thus—in loveliness! Bring no portion to me but thy love—'twill be generous in you Lydia—for well you know, it is the only dower your poor Beverley can repay.

LYDIA (*aside*) How persuasive are his words! How charming will poverty be with him.

ABSOLUTE (*aside*) Ah, my soul, what a life will we then live! [Love shall be our idol and support! We will worship him with a monastic strictness; abjuring all worldly toys, to centre every thought and action there. Proud of calamity, we will enjoy the wreck of wealth; while the surrounding gloom of adversity shall make the flame of our pure love show doubly bright.] By Heavens! I would fling all goods of fortune from me with a prodigal hand, to enjoy the scene where I might clasp my Lydia to my bosom, and say, the world affords no smile to me but here. (*He embraces her*) If she holds out now, the devil is in it.

LYDIA (*aside*) Now could I fly with him to the antipodes! But my persecution is not yet come to a crisis.

(MRS MALAPROP *enters up* C *from* R. *She stands listening*)

MRS MALAPROP (*aside*) I am impatient to know how the little hussy deports herself.

ABSOLUTE. So pensive, Lydia! Is, then, your warmth abated?

MRS MALAPROP (*aside*) Warmth abated! So! She has been in a passion, I suppose.

LYDIA. No, nor ever can while I have life.

MRS MALAPROP (*aside*) An ill-tempered little devil! She'll be in a passion all her life—will she?

LYDIA. Think not the idle threats of my ridiculous aunt can ever have any weight with me.

MRS MALAPROP (*aside*) Very dutiful, upon my word!

LYDIA. Let her choice be Captain Absolute, but Beverley is mine.

MRS MALAPROP (*aside*) I am astonished at her assurance! To his face—this is to his face!

ABSOLUTE (*kneeling*) Thus let me enforce my suit.

MRS MALAPROP (*aside*) Ay, poor young man! Down on his knees entreating for pity! I can contain no longer. (*Coming forward down* LC) Why, thou vixen! I have overheard you.

ABSOLUTE (*aside*) Oh, confound her vigilance!

MRS MALAPROP. Captain Absolute, I know not how to apologize for her shocking rudeness.

ABSOLUTE (*aside*) So all's safe, I find. (*Aloud*) I have hopes, madam, that time will bring the young lady . . .

MRS MALAPROP. Oh, there's nothing to be hoped for from her! She's as headstrong as an allegory on the banks of Nile.

LYDIA. Nay, madam, what do you charge me with now!

MRS MALAPROP. Why, thou unblushing rebel—didn't you tell this gentleman to his face that you loved another better? Didn't you say you never would be his?

LYDIA. No, madam—I did not.

MRS MALAPROP. Good heavens! What assurance! Lydia, Lydia, you ought to know that lying don't become a young woman! Didn't you boast that Beverley, that stroller Beverley, possessed your heart? Tell me that, I say.

LYDIA. 'Tis true, ma'am, and none but Beverley . . .

MRS MALAPROP. Hold! Hold! Assurance! You will not be so rude.

ABSOLUTE. Nay, pray, Mrs Malaprop, don't stop the young lady's speech: she's very welcome to talk thus—it does not hurt *me* in the least, I assure you.

MRS MALAPROP. You are *too* good, Captain—*too* amiably

patient—but come with me, miss. Let us see you again soon, Captain—remember what we have fixed.

ABSOLUTE. I shall, ma'am.

MRS MALAPROP. Come, take a graceless leave of the gentleman.

LYDIA. May every blessing wait on my Beverley, my loved Bev . . .

(MRS MALAPROP *claps a hand over Lydia's mouth, takes her by the right hand and, pulling her round, leads her up* C)

MRS MALAPROP. Hussy! I'll choke the word in your throat! Come along—come along.

(MRS MALAPROP *takes her hand from Lydia's mouth.* LYDIA *turns to the opening and gives a sly look at Absolute.* ABSOLUTE *kisses his hand to her.*

MRS MALAPROP *drags* LYDIA *off* R.

ABSOLUTE *exits* L)

SCENE 4

SCENE—*Acres' lodgings.*

ACRES *is discovered sitting at the dressing-table.* DAVID *is up* RC. ACRES *rises and moves a little down* R, *showing his clothes to David.*

ACRES. Indeed, David—do you think I become it so?

DAVID. You are quite another creature, believe me, master, by the mass! An' we've any luck we shall see the Devon monkerony in all the print-shops in Bath!

ACRES. Dress *does* make a difference, David.

DAVID. 'Tis all in all, I think. Difference! Why, an' you were to go now to Clod-Hall, I am certain the old lady wouldn't know you: Master Butler wouldn't believe his own eyes, and Mrs Pickle would cry, "Lard presarve me!"; our dairy-maid would come giggling to the door, and I warrant Dolly Tester, your honour's favourite, would blush like my waistcoat. Oons! I'll hold a gallon, there an't a dog in the house but would bark, and I question whether Phillis would wag a hair of her tail!

ACRES (*displaying his boots*) Ay, David, there's nothing like polishing.

DAVID. So I says of your honour's boots; but the boy never heeds me!

ACRES. But, David, has Mr De-la-grace been here? I must rub up my balancing, and chasing, and boring.

DAVID (*crossing* L) I'll call again, sir.

ACRES (*moving* C, *below the table*) Do—and see if there are any letters for me at the post-office.

DAVID (*turning to him*) I will. By the mass, I can't help looking at your head! If I hadn't been by at the cooking, I wish I may die if I should have known the dish again myself!

(DAVID *exits* L)

ACRES (*practising a dancing step*) Sink, slide—coupee. Confound the first inventors of cotillons, say I! They are as bad as algebra to us country gentlemen. I can walk a minuet easy enough when I am forced! And I have been accounted a good stick in a country-dance. Odds jigs and tabors! I never valued your cross-over to couple—figure in—right and left—and I'd foot it with e'er a captain in the county! But these outlandish heathen allemandes and cotillons are quite beyond me! I shall never prosper at 'em, that's sure—mine are true-born English legs—they don't understand their curst French lingo—their *pas* this, and *pas* that, and *pas* t'other! D—n me! My feet don't like to be called paws! No, 'tis certain I have most Antigallican toes!

(*A* SERVANT *enters* L)

SERVANT. Here is Sir Lucius O'Trigger to wait on you, sir.
ACRES. Show him in.

(*The* SERVANT *exits.*
        SIR LUCIUS O'TRIGGER *enters* L. *He crosses to* C *to meet Acres*)

SIR LUCIUS. Mr Acres, I am delighted to embrace you.
ACRES. My dear Sir Lucius, I kiss your hands.*
SIR LUCIUS (*laying his cane across the front of the table and his hat on the downstage* L *corner*) Pray, my friend, what has brought you so suddenly to Bath?
ACRES. Faith! I have followed Cupid's Jack-a-lantern, and find myself in a quagmire at last. In short, I have been very ill used, Sir Lucius. I don't choose to mention names, but look on me as on a very ill-used gentleman.
SIR LUCIUS. Pray what is the case? I ask no names.
ACRES. Mark me, Sir Lucius, I fall as deep as need be in love with a young lady—her friends take my part—I follow her to Bath—send word of my arrival; and receive answer, that the lady is to be otherwise disposed of. This, Sir Lucius, I call being ill used.
SIR LUCIUS. Very ill, upon my conscience. Pray, can you divine the cause of it?
ACRES. Why, there's the matter; she has another lover, one Beverley, who, I am told, is now in Bath. Odds slanders and lies! He must be at the bottom of it.
SIR LUCIUS. A rival in the case, is there? And you think he has supplanted you unfairly?
ACRES. Unfairly! To be sure he has. (*Moving down* R) He never could have done it fairly.

* This is merely a phrase of courteous salutation, and is not to be taken literally.

SIR LUCIUS. Then sure you know what is to be done!

ACRES (*moving up* R) Not I, upon my soul!

SIR LUCIUS. We wear no swords here, but you understand me.

ACRES (*turning sharply*) What! Fight him!

SIR LUCIUS. Ay, to be sure: what can I mean else?

ACRES (*coming down* R) But he has given me no provocation.

SIR LUCIUS. Now, I think he has given you the greatest provocation in the world. Can a man commit a more heinous offence against another than to fall in love with the same woman? Oh, by my soul, it is the most unpardonable breach of friendship.

ACRES. Breach of friendship! Ay, ay. But I have no acquaintance with this man. I never saw him in my life.

SIR LUCIUS. That's no argument at all—he has the less right then to take such a liberty.

ACRES. Gad, that's true. (*Crossing to* LC *and back again*) I grow full of anger, Sir Lucius! I fire apace! Odds hilts and blades! I find a man may have a deal of valour in him, and not know it! But couldn't I contrive to have a little right of my side?

SIR LUCIUS. What the devil signifies *right*, when your *honour* is concerned! Do you think Achilles, or my little Alexander the Great, ever inquired where the right lay! No, by my soul, they drew their broadswords, and left the lazy sons of peace to settle the justice of it.

ACRES. Your words are a grenadier's march to my heart! I believe courage must be catching! I certainly do feel a kind of valour rising as it were—a kind of courage, as I may say. (*Moving up* C *above the table*) Odds flints, pans, and triggers! I'll challenge him directly.

SIR LUCIUS (*moving up* L *of the table*) Ah, my little friend, if I had *Blunderbuss Hall* here I could show you a range of ancestry, in the O'Trigger line, that would furnish the New Room; every one of whom had killed his man! For though the mansion-house and dirty acres have slipt through my fingers, I thank Heaven our honour and the family pictures are as fresh as ever.

ACRES. O, Sir Lucius! I have had ancestors too! Every man of 'em colonel or captain—in the militia! Odds balls and barrels! Say no more—I'm braced for it. The thunder of your words has soured the milk of human kindness in my breast. Zounds! As the man in the play says, *I could do such deeds!* . . .

SIR LUCIUS (*sitting sideways on the* L *side of the table*) Come, come, there must be no passion at all in the case—these things should always be done civilly.

ACRES (*striking the table*) I must be in a passion, Sir Lucius— (*he strikes it again*) I must be in a rage. Dear Sir Lucius, let me be in a rage, if you love me. Come, here's pen and paper. (*He sits down to write*) I would the ink were red! Indite—I say, indite! How shall I begin? Odds bullets and blades! I'll write a good bold hand, however.

Sir Lucius. Pray compose yourself.

Acres. Come—now, shall I begin with an oath? Do, Sir Lucius, let me begin with a damme.

Sir Lucius. Pho! Pho! Do the thing decently, and like a Christian. Begin now—*Sir*——

Acres. That's too civil by half.

Sir Lucius. —*To prevent the confusion that might arise*——

Acres. Well . . .

Sir Lucius. —*from our both addressing the same lady*——

Acres. Ay, there's the reason—"*same lady*"—well . . .

Sir Lucius. —*I shall expect the honour of your company*——

Acres. Zounds! I'm not asking him to dinner.

Sir Lucius. Pray be easy.

Acres. Well, then, "*honour of your company*"——

Sir Lucius. *To settle our pretensions*——

Acres. Well.

Sir Lucius. Let me see, ay, King's-Mead-Fields will do—*in King's-Mead-Fields*.

Acres. So, that's done. Well, I'll fold it up presently: my own crest—a hand and dagger—shall be the seal.

Sir Lucius. You see now this little explanation will put a stop at once to all confusion or misunderstanding that might arise between you.

Acres. Ay, we fight to prevent any misunderstanding.

Sir Lucius (*rising and taking his hat and cane from the table and moving* LC) Now, I'll leave you to fix your own time. Take my advice, and you'll decide it this evening if you can; then let the worst come of it, 'twill be off your mind tomorrow.

Acres (*rising*) Very true.

Sir Lucius. So I shall see nothing more of you, unless it be by letter, till the evening. I would do myself the honour to carry your message; but to tell you a secret, I believe I shall have just such another affair on my own hands. There is a gay captain here, who put a jest on me lately, at the expense of my country, and I only want to fall in with the gentleman, to call him out.

Acres (*moving* R *of the table*) By my valour, I should like to see you fight first! Odds life! I should like to see you kill him, if it was only to get a little lesson.

Sir Lucius. I shall be very proud of instructing you. Well, for the present—but remember now, when you meet your antagonist, do everything in a mild and agreeable manner. Let your courage be as keen, but at the same time as polished, as your sword.

(Sir Lucius *exits* L.
    Acres *exits* R)

ACT IV

SCENE 1

SCENE—*Acres' lodgings.*

ACRES *is discovered sitting above the table with some sealing-wax held in a candle flame.* DAVID *is standing* L *of the table.*

DAVID. Then, by the mass, sir! I would do no such thing—ne'er a Sir Lucius O'Trigger in the kingdom should make me fight, when I wa'n't so minded. Oons! What will the old lady say, when she hears o't?

ACRES. Ah! David, if you had heard Sir Lucius! Odds sparks and flames! He would have roused your valour. (*He seals the letter and stamps it vigorously with his seal; then blows out the candle*)

DAVID. Not he, indeed. I hate such bloodthirsty cormorants. Look'ee, master, if you'd wanted a bout at boxing, quarter-staff, or short-staff, I should never be the man to bid you cry off: but for your curst sharps and snaps, I never knew any good come of 'em.

ACRES. But my honour, David, my honour! I must be very careful of my honour.

DAVID. Ay, by the mass! And I would be very careful of it; and I think in return my *honour* couldn't do less than to be very careful of *me*.

ACRES. Odds blades! David, no gentleman will ever risk the loss of his honour!

DAVID. I say then, it would be but civil in *honour* never to risk the loss of a *gentleman*. Look'ee, master, this *honour* seems to me to be a marvellous false friend: ay, truly, a very courtier-like servant. Put the case, I was a gentleman (which, thank God, no-one can say of me); well, my honour makes me quarrel with another of my acquaintance. So—we fight. (Pleasant enough that!) Boh! I kill him—(the more's my luck!) now, pray who gets the profit of it?—Why, my *honour*. But put the case that he kills me! By the mass! I go to the worms, and my honour whips over to my enemy.

ACRES. No, David—in that case—Odds crowns and laurels! Your honour follows you to the grave.

DAVID. Now, that's just the place where I could make a shift to do without it.

ACRES (*rising and moving* L *round the table, with the letter*) Zounds! David, you are a coward! It doesn't become my valour to listen to you. What, shall I disgrace my ancestors? Think of that, David —think what it would be to disgrace my ancestors!

DAVID. Under favour, the surest way of not disgracing them, is to keep as long as you can out of their company. (*Moving to Acres*) Look'ee now, master, to go to them in such haste—with an ounce of lead in your brains—I should think might as well be let alone. Our ancestors are very good kind of folks; but they are the last people I should choose to have a visiting acquaintance with.

ACRES. But, David, now you don't think there is such very, very, *very* great danger, hey? Odds life! People often fight without any mischief done!

DAVID. By the mass, I think 'tis ten to one against you! Oons! Here to meet some lion-headed fellow, I warrant, with his d—n'd double-barrelled swords, and cut-and-thrust pistols! Lord bless us! It makes me tremble to think o't! Those be such desperate bloody-minded weapons! Well, I never could abide 'em—from a child I never could fancy 'em! I suppose there an't been so merciless a beast in the world as your loaded pistol!

ACRES. Zounds! I *won't* be afraid! Odds fire and fury! You shan't make me afraid. (*Giving David the letter, holding it well away from him and backing a few steps*) Here is the challenge, and I have sent for my dear friend Jack Absolute to carry it for me.

DAVID. Ay, i' the name of mischief, let *him* be the messenger. For my part, I wouldn't lend a hand to it for the best horse in your stable. By the mass! It don't look like another letter! It is, as I may say, a designing and malicious-looking letter; and I warrant smells of gunpowder like a soldier's pouch! (*He drops the letter and backs across to* R, *looking apprehensively at it*) Oons! I wouldn't swear it mayn't go off!

ACRES. Out, you poltroon! You ha'n't the valour of a grasshopper.

DAVID. Well, I say no more—'twill be sad news, to be sure, at Clod-Hall! But I ha' done. How Phillis will howl when she hears of it! Ay, poor bitch, she little thinks what shooting her master's going after! And I warrant old Crop, who has carried your honour, field and road, these ten years, will curse the hour he was born.

ACRES. It won't do, David—I am determined to fight—so get along, you coward, while I'm in the mind. (*He picks up the letter*)

(*A* SERVANT *enters* R)

SERVANT. Captain Absolute, sir.
ACRES. Oh, show him up.

(*The* SERVANT *exits* R)

DAVID. Well, Heaven send we be all alive this time tomorrow.
ACRES. What's that? Don't provoke me, David!
DAVID (*whimpering*) Good-bye, master.
ACRES. Get along, you cowardly, dastardly, croaking raven!

(DAVID *exits* R.
ABSOLUTE *enters* R. *He carries a hat and cane. He crosses to* Acres)

ABSOLUTE. What's the matter, Bob?

ACRES. A vile, sheep-hearted blockhead! If I hadn't the valour of St George and the dragon to boot . . .

ABOLUTE. But what did you want of me, Bob?

ACRES. Oh . . . There . . . (*He thrusts the letter at Absolute*)

ABSOLUTE (*aside*) To Ensign Beverley. So, what's going on now! (*Aloud*) Well, what's this?

ACRES. A challenge!

ABSOLUTE. Indeed! Why, you won't fight him; will you, Bob?

ACRES. Egad, but I will, Jack. Sir Lucius has wrought me to it. He has left me full of rage—and I'll fight this evening, that so much good passion mayn't be wasted.

ABSOLUTE. But what have I to do with this?

ACRES. Why, as I think you know something of this fellow, I want you to find him out for me, and give him this mortal defiance.

ABSOLUTE. Well, give it to me, and trust me he gets it. (*He takes the letter*)

ACRES. Thank you, my dear friend, my dear Jack; but it is giving you a great deal of trouble.

ABSOLUTE. Not in the least—I beg you won't mention it. No trouble in the world, I assure you.

ACRES. You are very kind. What it is to have a friend! You couldn't be my second, could you, Jack?

ABSOLUTE. Why, no, Bob—not in *this* affair—it would not be quite so proper.

ACRES. Well, then, I must get my friend Sir Lucius! I shall have your good wishes, however, Jack?

ABSOLUTE. Whenever he meets you, believe me.

(*The* SERVANT *enters* R)

SERVANT. Sir Anthony Absolute is below, inquiring for the captain.

ABSOLUTE. I'll come instantly.

(*The* SERVANT *exits*)

Well, my little hero, success attend you. (*He moves to the door* R)

ACRES. Stay—stay, Jack. If Beverley should ask you what kind of a man your friend Acres is, do tell him I am a devil of a fellow —will you, Jack?

ABSOLUTE. To be sure I shall. (*Returning to Acres*) I'll say you are a determined dog—hey, Bob!

ACRES. Ay, do, do; and if that frightens him, egad, perhaps

he mayn't come. So tell him I generally kill a man a week; will you, Jack?

ABSOLUTE. I will, I will; I'll say you are called in the country *Fighting Bob.*

ACRES. Right, right—'tis all to prevent mischief; for I don't want to take his life if I clear my honour.

ABSOLUTE. No! That's very kind of you.

ACRES. Why, you don't wish me to kill him—do you, Jack?

ABSOLUTE. No, upon my soul, I do not. But a devil of a fellow, hey? (*He moves* R *towards the door*)

ACRES. True, true—but stay—stay, Jack—you may add, that you never saw me in such a rage before—a most devouring rage!

ABSOLUTE. I will, I will.

ACRES. Remember, Jack—a determined dog!

ABSOLUTE. Ay, ay, *Fighting Bob.*

(ABSOLUTE *exits* R)

SCENE 2

SCENE—*Mrs Malaprop's lodgings.*

MRS MALAPROP *and* LYDIA *enter up* C *from* R. *They come down* C, *Malaprop on the* R

MRS MALAPROP. Why, thou perverse one! Tell me what you can object to him? Isn't he a handsome man? Tell me that. A genteel man? A pretty figure of a man.

LYDIA (*aside*) She little thinks whom she is praising! (*Aloud*) So is Beverley, ma'am.

MRS MALAPROP. No caparisons, miss, if you please. Caparisons don't become a young woman. No! Captain Absolute is indeed a fine gentleman!

LYDIA (*aside*) Ay, the Captain Absolute *you* have seen.

MRS MALAPROP. Then he's *so* well bred—*so* full of alacrity, and adulation! And has *so much* to say for himself: in such good language too! His physiognomy so grammatical! Then his presence is so noble! I protest, when I saw him, I thought of what Hamlet says in the play:

> "Hesperian curls—the front of *Job* himself!—
> An eye, like *March*, to threaten at command!—
> A station, like Harry Mercury, new . . ."

Something about kissing—on a hill—however, the similitude struck me directly.

LYDIA (*aside*) How enraged she'll be presently, when she discovers her mistake!

(*A* SERVANT *enters* R)

SERVANT. Sir Anthony and Captain Absolute are below, ma'am.

MRS MALAPROP. Show them up here.

(*The* SERVANT *crosses and exits* L. LYDIA *moves to the armchair* RC. *She stands up* R *of it, facing down* R)

Now, Lydia, I insist on your behaving as becomes a young woman. Show your good breeding, at least, though you have forgot your duty.

LYDIA. Madam, I have told you my resolution! I shall not only give him no encouragement, but I won't even speak to or look at him. (*She flings herself into the chair, with her face turned from the door*)

(SIR ANTHONY *and* CAPTAIN ABSOLUTE *enter* L. *They do not carry hats or canes.* SIR ANTHONY *moves* LC *towards Mrs Malaprop.* ABSOLUTE *follows him, but stands* L *of him and faces a little away down* L)

SIR ANTHONY. Here we are, Mrs Malaprop; come to mitigate the frowns of unrelenting beauty; and difficulty enough I had to bring this fellow. I don't know what's the matter; but if I had not held him by force, he'd h_ave given me the slip.

MRS MALAPROP. You have infinite trouble, Sir Anthony, in the affair. I am ashamed for the cause! (*Aside to Lydia*) Lydia, Lydia, rise, I beseech you—pay your respects!

SIR ANTHONY. I hope, madam, that Miss Languish has reflected on the worth of this gentleman, and the regard due to her aunt's choice, and *my* alliance. (*Aside*) Now, Jack, speak to her.

ABSOLUTE. What the d—l shall I do! (*Aside to Sir Anthony*) You see, sir, she won't even look at me whilst you are here. I knew she wouldn't! I told you so. Let me entreat you, sir, to leave us together! (*He seems to expostulate with his father*)

LYDIA (*aside*) I wonder. I ha'n't heard my aunt exclaim yet! Sure she can't have looked at him! Perhaps their regimentals are alike, and she is something blind.

SIR ANTHONY. I say, sir, I won't stir a foot yet!

MRS MALAPROP. I am sorry to say, Sir Anthony, that my afflı ence over my niece is very small. (*She moves up to Lydia's chair and stands above* L *of it*) Turn round, Lydia: I blush for you!

SIR ANTHONY (*moving* C) May I not flatter myself, that Miss Languish will assign what cause of dislike she can have to my son? Why don't you begin, Jack? (*Aside to him*) Speak, you puppy— speak!

MRS MALAPROP. It is impossible, Sir Anthony, she can have any. She will not say she has. (*Aside to her*) Answer, hussy! Why don't you answer?

SIR ANTHONY. Then, madam, I trust that a childish and hasty

predilection will be no bar to Jack's happiness. (*Crossing to Absolute. Aside to him*) Zounds! sirrah! Why don't you speak?

LYDIA (*aside*) I think my lover seems as little inclined to conversation as myself. How strangely blind my aunt must be!

ABSOLUTE (*timorously crossing to* c) Hem! Hem! Madam—hem! (*He returns to Sir Anthony*) Faith, sir, I am so confounded! And—so—so—confused! I told you I should be so, sir—I knew it. (*He crosses* L. *Assuming an emotional confusion*) The—the—tremor of my passion entirely takes away my presence of mind.

SIR ANTHONY. But it don't take away your voice, fool, does it? Go up, and speak to her directly!

(ABSOLUTE *turns and makes signs to Mrs Malaprop to leave them together*)

MRS MALAPROP (*coming* c) Sir Anthony, shall we leave them together? (*Aside to Lydia*) Ah, you stubborn little vixen!

SIR ANTHONY. Not yet, ma'am, not yet! (*Aside to Absolute*) What the d—l are you at? Unlock your jaws, sirrah, or . . .

ABSOLUTE (*crossing hesitatingly towards Lydia; aside*) Now Heaven send she may be too sullen to look round! I must disguise my voice. (*He stands above her chair and speaks in a low hoarse tone*) Will not Miss Languish lend an ear to the mild accents of true love? Will not . . .

SIR ANTHONY. What the d—l ails the fellow! Why don't you speak out? Not stand croaking like a frog in a quinsy!

ABSOLUTE. The—the—excess of my awe, and my—my—my modesty quite choke me!

SIR ANTHONY. Ah! Your *modesty* again! I'll tell you what, Jack; if you *don't* speak out directly, and glibly too, I shall be in such a rage! Mrs Malaprop, I wish the lady would favour us with something more than a side-front.

(MRS MALAPROP *crosses to Lydia and speaks to her in dumb-show. Then she leaves her in disgust and returns to* c)

ABSOLUTE (*moving* R, *in front of Lydia; aside*) So all will out, I see! (*Softly*) Be not surprised, my Lydia—suppress all surprise at present.

LYDIA (*aside*) Heavens! 'Tis Beverley's voice! Sure he can't have imposed on Sir Anthony too! (*She looks round by degrees, then rises*) Is this possible! My Beverley! How can this be? My Beverley?

ABSOLUTE (*crossing down* R; *aside*) Ah! 'Tis all over.

SIR ANTHONY. Beverley! The devil—Beverley! What can the girl mean? This is my son, Jack Absolute.

MRS MALAPROP. For shame, hussy! For shame! Your head runs so on that fellow, that you have him always in your eyes! Beg Captain Absolute's pardon directly.

LYDIA. I see no Captain Absolute, but my loved Beverley!

Sir Anthony. Zounds! The girl's mad! Her brain's turned by reading.

Mrs Malaprop. O' my conscience, I believe so! (*With a step towards Lydia*) What do you mean by Beverley, hussy? You saw Captain Absolute before today; there he is—your husband that shall be.

Lydia. With all my soul, ma'am—when I refuse my Beverley.

Sir Anthony. Oh! She's as mad as Bedlam! Or has this fellow been playing us a rogue's trick! Come here, sirrah—who the d—l are you?

(Absolute *crosses to Sir Anthony*)

Absolute (*in comical confusion*) Faith, sir, I am not quite clear myself; but I'll endeavour to recollect.

Sir Anthony. Are you my son, or not? Answer for your mother, you dog, if you won't for me.

Mrs Malaprop (*coming down* R *of Absolute*) Ay, sir, who are you? Oh mercy! I begin to suspect!

Absolute (*aside*) Ye powers of impudence, befriend me! (*Aloud*) Sir Anthony, most assuredly I am your wife's son, and that I sincerely believe myself to be *yours* also, I hope my duty has always been shown. Mrs Malaprop, I am your most respectful admirer, and shall be proud to add affectionate nephew. I need not tell my Lydia, that she sees her faithful Beverley, who, knowing the singular generosity of her temper, assumed that name and station, which has proved a test of the most disinterested love, which he now hopes to enjoy in a more elevated character.

Lydia (*sullenly*) So! There will be no elopement after all! (*She swirls round to* RC)

Sir Anthony (*moving to Absolute*) Upon my soul, Jack, thou art a very impudent fellow! To do you justice, I think I never saw a piece of more consummate assurance!

Absolute. Oh, you flatter me, sir—you compliment—'tis my *modesty*, you know, sir—my *modesty* that has stood in my way.

Sir Anthony. Well, I am glad you are not the dull, insensible varlet you pretended to be, however! I'm glad you have made a fool of your father, you dog—I am. So this was your *penitence*, your *duty* and *obedience!* I thought it was d—d sudden! *You never heard their names before*, not you! *What, the Languishes of Worcestershire*, hey? *If you could please me in the affair it was all you desired!* Ah! You dissembling villain! What! (*Pointing to Lydia*) She *squints, don't she? A little red-haired girl!* Hey? Why, you hypocritical rascal! I wonder you an't ashamed to hold up your head!

Absolute. 'Tis with difficulty, sir. I *am* confused—very much confused, as you must perceive.

Mrs Malaprop. Oh Lud! Sir Anthony! A new light breaks in upon me! Hey! How! What! Captain, did *you* write the letters then! What—am I to thank *you* for the elegant compilation of "*an old weather-beaten she-dragon*"—hey! Oh mercy! Was it *you* that reflected on my parts of speech!

ABSOLUTE. Dear sir, my modesty will be overpowered at last, if you don't assist me—I shall certainly not be able to stand it! (*He moves up* L *to the window*)

SIR ANTHONY. Come, come, Mrs Malaprop, we must forget and forgive. Odds life! Matters have taken so clever a turn all of a sudden, that I could find in my heart to be so good-humoured! And so gallant! Hey! Mrs Malaprop!

MRS MALAPROP. Well, Sir Anthony, since *you* desire it, we will not anticipate the past! So mind, young people—our retrospection will be all to the future.

SIR ANTHONY. Come, we must leave them together, Mrs Malaprop, they long to fly into each other's arms, I warrant!

(ABSOLUTE *comes down* L)

Jack—isn't the cheek as I said, hey? And the eye, you rogue! And the lip—hey? Come, Mrs Malaprop, we'll not disturb their tenderness—theirs is the time of life for happiness! (*He sings*) "Youth's the season made for joy." Hey! Odds life! I'm in such spirits. I don't know what I could not do! Permit me, ma'am. (*He gives his hand to Mrs Malaprop*) Tol-de-rol. Gad, I should like to have a little fooling myself. Tol-de-rol, de-rol!

(SIR ANTHONY *exits up* C *to* R, *singing, and handing* MRS MALA-PROP. LYDIA *moves to the chair* RC *and sits sullenly*)

ABSOLUTE (*aside*) So much thought bodes me no good. (*Moving* C. *Aloud*) So grave, Lydia?

LYDIA. Sir!

ABSOLUTE (*aside*) So! Egad! I thought as much! That d—d monosyllable has froze me! (*Going to her. Aloud*) What, Lydia, now that we are as happy in our friends' consent, as in our mutual vows . . .

LYDIA (*peevishly*) *Friends' consent*, indeed!

ABSOLUTE. Come, come, we must lay aside some of our romance —a little *wealth* and *comfort* may be endured after all. And for your fortune, the lawyers shall make such settlements as . . .

LYDIA. *Lawyers!* I hate lawyers!

ABSOLUTE. Nay, then, we will not wait for their lingering forms, but instantly procure the licence, and . . .

LYDIA. The *licence!* I hate licence!

ABSOLUTE (*kneeling*) Oh, my love, be not so unkind! Thus let me entreat . . .

LYDIA. Psha! What signifies kneeling, when you know I *must* have you?

ABSOLUTE (*rising*) Nay, madam, there shall be no constraint upon your inclinations, I promise you. If I have lost your heart

—I resign the rest. (*Moving* C. *Aside*) Gad, I must try what a little spirit will do.

LYDIA (*rising*) Then, sir, let me tell you, the interest you had there was acquired by a mean, unmanly imposition, and deserves the punishment of fraud. What, you have been treating *me* like a child! Humouring my romance! And laughing, I suppose, at your success!

ABSOLUTE. You wrong me, Lydia, you wrong me—only hear ...

LYDIA. So, while *I* fondly imagined we were deceiving my relations, and flattered myself that I would outwit and incense them all—behold my hopes are to be crushed at once, by my aunt's consent and approbation—and *I* am myself the only dupe at last! (*Walking up and down in a rage*) But here, sir, here is the picture—Beverley's picture—(*taking a miniature from her bosom*) which I have worn, night and day, in spite of threats and entreaties! There, sir! (*She flings it to him*) And be assured I throw the original from my heart as easily.

ABSOLUTE. Nay, nay, ma'am, we will not differ as to that. Here—(*taking out a picture*) here is Miss Lydia Languish. What a difference! Ay, *there* is the heavenly assenting smile that first gave soul and spirit to my hopes! Those are the lips which sealed a vow, as yet scarce dry in Cupid's calendar! And there the half-resentful blush, that would have checked the ardour of my thanks! Well, all that's past! All over indeed! There, madam—in beauty that copy is not equal to you, but in my mind its merit over the original, in being still the same, is such—that—I cannot find in my heart to part with it. (*He puts it up again*)

LYDIA (*softening*) 'Tis *your own* doing, sir—I—I—I suppose you are perfectly satisfied.

ABSOLUTE. Oh, most certainly—sure, now, this is much better than being in love! Ha! Ha! Ha! There's some spirit in *this!* What signifies breaking some scores of solemn promises: all that's of no consequence, you know. To be sure people will say, that miss didn't know her own mind—but never mind that! Or, perhaps, they may be ill-natured enough to hint, that the gentleman grew tired of the lady, and forsook her—but don't let that fret you. (*He comes* L, *very airily*)

LYDIA. There is no bearing his insolence. (*She bursts into tears*)

(MRS MALAPROP *and* SIR ANTHONY *enter up* C)

MRS MALAPROP. Come, we must interrupt your billing and cooing awhile.

LYDIA. This is worse than your treachery and deceit, you base ingrate! (*She sits in the chair* RC *and sobs*)

SIR ANTHONY. What the devil's the matter now? Zounds, Mrs Malaprop, this is the oddest *billing and cooing* I ever heard! But what the deuce is the meaning of it? I am quite astonished.

ABSOLUTE. Ask the lady, sir.

MRS MALAPROP. Oh mercy! I'm quite analysed, for my part! Why, Lydia, what is the reason of this?

LYDIA. Ask the gentleman, ma'am.

SIR ANTHONY. Zounds! I shall be in a frenzy! Why, Jack, you are not come out to be anyone else, are you?

MRS MALAPROP. Ay, sir, there's no more trick, is there? You are not like Cerberus, *three* gentlemen at once, are you?

ABSOLUTE. You'll not let me speak—I say the lady can account for this much better than I can.

LYDIA (*rising*) Ma'am, you once commanded me never to think of Beverley again; there is the man—I now obey you: for, from this moment, I renounce him for ever.

(LYDIA *exits* R)

MRS MALAPROP. Oh mercy, and miracles! What a turn here is! Why sure, Captain, you haven't behaved disrespectfully to my niece.

SIR ANTHONY. Ha! Ha! Ha! Ha! Ha! Ha! Now I see it—you have been too lively, Jack.

ABSOLUTE. Nay, sir, upon my word . . .

SIR ANTHONY. Come, no lying, Jack—I'm sure '*twas* so.

MRS MALAPROP. Oh Lud! Sir Anthony! Oh fie, Captain!

ABSOLUTE. Upon my soul, ma'am . . .

SIR ANTHONY. Come, no excuses, Jack; why, your father, you rogue, was so before you: the blood of the Absolutes was always impatient. Ha! Ha! Ha! Poor little Lydia! Why, you've frightened her, you dog, you have.

ABSOLUTE. By all that's good, sir . . .

SIR ANTHONY. Zounds! Say no more, I tell you. Mrs Malaprop shall make your peace. You must make his peace, Mrs Malaprop: you must tell her 'tis Jack's way. Tell her 'tis all our ways—it runs in the blood of our family! Come away, Jack. Ha! Ha! Ha! Mrs Malaprop—a young villain!

MRS MALAPROP. Oh, Sir Anthony! Oh fie, Captain!

(SIR ANTHONY *exits* L, *pushing* ABSOLUTE *before him.* MRS MALAPROP *stands staring after them*)

SCENE 3

SCENE—*The North Parade.*

SIR LUCIUS O'TRIGGER *enters* R.

SIR LUCIUS. I wonder where this Captain Absolute hides himself. Upon my conscience, these officers are always in one's way in love affairs. I remember I might have married Lady Dorothy Carmine, if it had not been for a little rogue of a major, who ran away with her before she could get a sight of me! And I wonder, too, what it is the ladies can see in them to be so fond of them— unless it be a touch of the old serpent in 'em, that makes the little creatures be caught, like vipers, with a bit of red cloth. Ha! Isn't this the captain coming? Faith it is! There is a probability of suc- ceeding about that fellow, that is mighty provoking! Who the devil is he talking to? (*He steps aside, and stands up* R *against the trailers*)

(CAPTAIN ABSOLUTE *enters* L. *He comes* LC, *very much occupied with his own thoughts*)

ABSOLUTE (*aside*) To what fine purpose I have been plotting! A noble reward for all my schemes upon my soul! A little gypsy! I did not think her romance could have made her so d—d absurd either. 'Sdeath, I never was in a worse humour in my life! I could cut my own throat, or any other person's, with the greatest pleasure in the world!

SIR LUCIUS (*aside*) Oh faith! I'm in the luck of it. I never could have found him in a sweeter temper for my purpose. To be sure I'm just come in the nick! Now to enter into conversation with him, and so quarrel genteelly. (*Coming* C) With regard to that matter, Captain, I must beg leave to differ in opinion with you.

ABSOLUTE (*distantly*) Upon my word, then, you must be a very subtle disputant: because, sir, I happened just then to be giving no opinion at all.

SIR LUCIUS. That's no reason. For give me leave to tell you, a man may *think* an untruth as well as speak one.

ABSOLUTE. Very true, sir; but if a man never utters his thoughts I should think they might stand a chance of escaping controversy.

SIR LUCIUS. Then, sir, you differ in opinion with me, which amounts to the same thing.

ABSOLUTE (*moving to him*) Hark'ee, Sir Lucius: if I had not before known you to be a gentleman, upon my soul, I should not have discovered it at this interview; for what you can drive at, unless you mean to quarrel with me, I cannot conceive!

SIR LUCIUS. I humbly thank you, sir, for the quickness of your apprehension. (*He bows*) You have named the very thing I would be at.

ABSOLUTE. Very well, sir; I shall certainly not balk your inclinations. But I should be glad you would please to explain your motives.

SIR LUCIUS. Pray, sir, be easy; the quarrel is a very pretty quarrel as it stands; we should only spoil it by trying to explain it. However, your memory is very short, or you could not have forgot an affront you passed on me within this week. So, no more, but name your time and place.

ABSOLUTE. Well, sir, since you are so bent on it, the sooner the better; let it be this evening—here, by the Spring Gardens. We shall scarcely be interrupted.

Sir Lucius. Faith! That same interruption in affairs of this nature shows very great ill breeding. I don't know what's the reason, but in England, if a thing of this kind gets wind, people make such a pother, that a gentleman can never fight in peace and quietness. However, if it's the same to you, Captain, I should take it as a particular kindness if you'd let us meet in King's-Mead-Fields, as a little business will call me there about six o'clock, and I may dispatch both matters at once.

Absolute. 'Tis the same to me exactly. A little after six, then, we will discuss this matter more seriously.

Sir Lucius. If you please, sir; there will be very pretty small-sword light, though it won't do for a long shot. So that matter's settled, and my mind's at ease!

(Sir Lucius *exits* R.
Faulkland *enters* L)

Absolute. Well met! I was going to look for you. Oh, Faulkland, all the demons of spite and disappointment have conspired against me! I'm so vexed, that if I had not the prospect of a resource in being knocked o' the head by and by, I should scarce have spirits to tell you the cause.

Faulkland. What can you mean? Has Lydia changed her mind? I should have thought her duty and inclination would now have pointed to the same object.

Absolute. Ay, just as the eyes do of a person who squints: when her love-eye was fixed on me, t'other, her eye of duty, was finely obliqued: but when duty bid her point that the same way, off t'other turned on a swivel, and secure its retreat with a frown!

Faulkland. But what's the resource you . . .

Absolute. Oh, to wind up the whole, a good-natured Irishman here has—(*mimicking Sir Lucius*) begged leave to have the pleasure of cutting my throat; and I mean to indulge him—that's all.

Faulkland. Prithee, be serious!

Absolute. 'Tis fact, upon my soul! Sir Lucius O'Trigger—you know him by sight—for some affront, which I am sure I never intended, has obliged me to meet him this evening at six o'clock: 'tis on that account I wished to see you; you must go with me.

Faulkland. Nay, there must be some mistake, sure. Sir Lucius shall explain himself, and I dare say matters may be accommodated. But this evening did you say? I wish it had been at any other time.

Absolute. Why, there will be light enough; there will—as Sir Lucius says—be a very pretty small-sword light, though it will not do for a long shot. Confound his long shots!

Faulkland. But I am myself a good deal ruffled by a difference I have had with Julia. My vile tormenting temper has made me treat her so cruelly, that I shall not be myself till we are reconciled.

ABSOLUTE. By heavens, Faulkland, you don't deserve her!

(*A* SERVANT *enters* L, *gives Faulkland a letter, and exits*)

FAULKLAND. Oh, Jack, this is from Julia. I dread to open it! I fear it may be to take a last leave. Perhaps to bid me return her letters, and restore . . . Oh, how I suffer for my folly!

ABSOLUTE. Here, let me see. (*He takes the letter and opens it*)

(FAULKLAND *turns away to* L, *and waits apprehensively*)

Ay, a final sentence, indeed! 'Tis all over with you, faith!

FAULKLAND. Nay, Jack, don't keep me in suspense!

ABSOLUTE. Hear then: "As I am convinced that my dear Faulkland's own reflections have already upbraided him for his last unkindness to me, I will not add a word on the subject. I wish to speak with you as soon as possible. Yours ever and truly Julia." There's stubbornness and resentment for you!

(FAULKLAND *turns, goes quickly to Absolute and takes the letter*)

Why, man, you don't seem one whit the happier at this!

FAULKLAND. Oh, yes, I am; but—but . . .

ABSOLUTE. Confound your *buts!* You never hear anything that would make another man bless himself, but you immediately d—n it with a *but!*

FAULKLAND. [Now, Jack, as you are my friend, own honestly— don't you think there is something forward, something indelicate in this haste to forgive! Women should never sue for reconciliation: that should always come from us. They should retain their cold- ness till *wooed* to kindness; and their *pardon*, like their *love*, should "not unsought be won."]

ABSOLUTE (*abruptly crossing to* LC) I have not patience to listen to you! (*Turning*) Thou'rt incorrigible, so say no more on the subject. I must go to settle a few matters. Let me see you before six, remember, at my lodgings. A poor industrious devil like me, who have toiled, and drudged, and plotted to gain my ends, and am at last disappointed by other people's folly, may in pity be allowed to swear a little; but a captious sceptic in love, a slave of fretfulness and whim, who has no difficulties but of his own creating, is a subject more for ridicule than compassion!

(ABSOLUTE *exits* L)

FAULKLAND. I feel his reproaches; yet I would not change this too exquisite nicety for the gross content with which *he* tramples on the thorns of love! His engaging me in this duel has started an idea in my head, which I will instantly pursue. I'll use it as the touchstone of Julia's sincerity and disinterestedness. If her love prove pure and sterling ore, my name will rest on it with honour; and once I've stamped it there, I lay aside my doubts for ever! But if the dross of selfishness, the alloy of pride, predominate, 'twill be best to leave her as a toy for some less cautious fool to sigh for!

(FAULKLAND *exits* L)

ACT V

SCENE I

SCENE—*Julia's dressing-room.*

JULIA *is discovered standing* C, *reading a letter.*

JULIA. How this message has alarmed me! What dreadful accident can he mean? Why such charge to be alone? Oh, Faulkland—how many unhappy moments—how many tears have you cost me!

(FAULKLAND *enters* L, *and crosses to* LC)

What means this? Why this caution, Faulkland?

FAULKLAND. Alas! Julia, I am come to take a long farewell.

JULIA. Heavens! What do you mean!

FAULKLAND. You see before you a wretch, whose life is forfeited. Nay, start not! The infirmity of my temper has drawn all this misery on me. I left you fretful and passionate—an untoward accident drew me into a quarrel—the event is, that I must fly this kingdom instantly. Oh, Julia, had I been so fortunate as to have called you mine entirely, before this mischance had fallen on me, I should not so deeply dread my banishment.

JULIA. My soul is oppressed with sorrow at the nature of your misfortune: had these adverse circumstances arisen from a less fatal cause, I should have felt strong comfort in the thought that I could now chase from your bosom every doubt of the warm sincerity of my love. My heart has long known no other guardian —(*moving close to him*) I now entrust my person to your honour— we will fly together. When safe from pursuit, my father's will may be fulfilled—and I receive a legal claim to be the partner of your sorrows, and tenderest comforter. [Then on the bosom of your wedded Julia, you may lull your keen regret to slumbering; while virtuous love, with a cherub's hand, shall smooth the brow of upbraiding thought, and pluck the thorn from compunction.]

FAULKLAND. Oh, Julia! I am bankrupt in gratitude! But the time is so pressing, it calls on you for so hasty a resolution. [Would you not wish some hours to weigh the advantages you forego, and what little compensation poor Faulkland can make you beside his solitary love?]

JULIA. I ask not a moment. No, Faulkland, I have loved you for yourself: and if I now, more than ever, prize the solemn engagement which so long pledged us to each other, it is because it leaves no room for hard aspersions on my frame, and puts the seal of duty to an act of love. But let us not linger. Perhaps this delay . . .

[FAULKLAND. 'Twill be better I should not venture out again till dark. Yet I am grieved to think what numberless distresses will press heavy on your gentle disposition.

JULIA. Perhaps your fortune may be forfeited by this unhappy act. I know not whether 'tis so; but sure that alone can never make us unhappy. The little I have will be sufficient to support us; and exile never should be splendid.

FAULKLAND. Ay, but in such an abject state of life, my wounded pride perhaps may increase the natural fretfulness of my temper, till I become a rude, morose companion, beyond your patience to endure. Perhaps the recollection of a deed my conscience cannot justify may haunt me in such gloomy and unsocial fits, that I shall hate the tenderness that would relieve me, break from your arms, and quarrel with your fondness.

JULIA. If your thoughts should assume so unhappy a bent, you will the more want some mild and affectionate spirit to watch over and console you: one who, by bearing your infirmities with gentleness and resignation, may teach you so to bear the evils of your fortune.]

FAULKLAND. Julia, I have proved you to the quick! And with this useless device I throw away all my doubts. How shall I plead to be forgiven this last unworthy effect of my restless, unsatisfied disposition?

JULIA. Has no such disaster happened as you related?

FAULKLAND (*turning away a little down* L) I am ashamed to own that it was pretended; yet in pity, Julia, do not kill me with resenting a fault which never can be repeated: but sealing, this once, my pardon, let me tomorrow, in the face of Heaven, receive my future guide and monitress, and expiate my past folly by years of tender adoration.

JULIA. Hold, Faulkland! That you are free from a crime, which I before feared to name, Heaven knows how sincerely I rejoice! These are tears of thankfulness for that! But that your cruel doubts should have urged you to an imposition that has wrung my heart, gives me now a pang more keen than I can express!

FAULKLAND (*turning*) By Heavens, Julia . . .

JULIA. Yet hear me. My father loved you, Faulkland! And you preserved the life that tender parent gave me; in his presence I pledged my hand—joyfully pledged it—where before I had given my heart. When, soon after, I lost that parent, it seemed to me that Providence had, in Faulkland, shown me whither to transfer without a pause my grateful duty, as well as my affection: hence I have been content to bear from you what pride and delicacy would have forbid me from another. I will not upbraid you, by repeating how you have trifled with my sincerity . . .

FAULKLAND. I confess it all. Yet hear . . .

JULIA. After such a year of trial, I might have flattered myself that I should not have been insulted with a new probation of my sincerity, as cruel as unnecessary! I now see it is not in your nature to be content or confident in love. With this conviction— I never will be yours. [While I had hopes that my persevering attention, and unreproaching kindness, might in time reform your temper, I should have been happy to have gained a dearer influence over you; but] I will not furnish you with a licensed power to keep alive an incorrigible fault at the expense of one who never would contend with you. (*She turns away up* C, *in front of the sofa*)

FAULKLAND. Nay, but, Julia, by my soul and honour, if after this . . .

JULIA (*turning to him*) But one word more. As my faith has once been given to you, I never will barter it with another. I shall pray for your happiness with the truest sincerity; and the dearest blessing I can ask of Heaven to send you will be to charm you from that unhappy temper, which alone has prevented the per- formance of our solemn engagement. (*She moves to the door* R, *and turns*) All I request of *you* is, that you will yourself reflect upon this infirmity, and when you number up the true delights it has de- prived you of, let it not be your *least* regret, that it lost you the love of one who would have followed you in beggary through the world.

(JULIA *exits* R)

FAULKLAND. She's gone—for ever! There was an awful resolu- tion in her manner, that riveted me to my place. (*Moving down* L) Oh, fool! Dolt! Barbarian! Curst as I am, with more imperfec- tions than my fellow wretches, kind Fortune sent a heaven-gifted cherub to my aid, and, like, a ruffian, I have driven her from my side! I must now haste to my appointment. Well, my mind is tuned for such a scene. I shall wish only to become a principal in it, and reverse the tale my cursed folly put me upon forging here. Oh Love! Tormentor! Fiend—whose influence, like the moon's, acting on men of dull souls, makes idiots of them, but meeting subtler spirits, betrays their course, and urges sensibility to madness!

(FAULKLAND *exits* L.
    LYDIA *and a* MAID *enter* R)

MAID. My mistress, ma'am, I know, was here, just now— perhaps she is only in the next room.

(*The* MAID *exits* R)

LYDIA (*crossing to* C) Heigh-ho! Though he has used me so, this fellow runs strangely in my head. I believe one lecture from my grave cousin will make me recall him.

(JULIA *enters* R)

Oh, Julia, I am come to you with such an appetite for consolation. Lud, child, what's the matter with you? You have been crying! I'll be hanged if that Faulkland has not been tormenting you!

JULIA. You mistake the cause of my uneasiness. (*Crossing in front of the sofa, and sitting*) Something *has* flurried me a little. Nothing that you can guess at. (*Aside*) I would not accuse Faulkland to a sister.

LYDIA (*sitting beside Julia*) Ah! Whatever vexations you may have, I can assure you mine surpass them. You know who Beverley proves to be?

JULIA. I will now own to you, Lydia, that Mr Faulkland had before informed me of the whole affair. Had young Absolute been the person you took him for, I should not have accepted your confidence on the subject, without a serious endeavour to counteract your caprice.

LYDIA. So, then, I see I have been deceived by everyone! But I don't care—I'll never have him.

JULIA. Nay, Lydia . . .

LYDIA. Why, is it not provoking? When I thought we were coming to the prettiest distress imaginable, to find myself made a mere Smithfield bargain of at last! There had I projected one of the most sentimental elopements! So becoming a disguise! So amiable a ladder of ropes! Conscious moon—four horses—Scotch parson—with such surprise to Mrs Malaprop—and such paragraphs in the newspapers! (*Rising and crossing to* RC) Oh, I shall die with disappointment!

JULIA. I don't wonder at it!

LYDIA. Now—sad reverse! What have I to expect, but, after a deal of flimsy preparation, with a bishop's licence and my aunt's blessing, to go simpering up to the altar; or perhaps be cried three times in a country church, and have an unmannerly fat clerk ask the consent of every butcher in the parish to join John Absolute and Lydia Languish, spinster! (*Crossing to* LC) Oh, that I should live to hear myself called spinster!

JULIA. Melancholy, indeed!

LYDIA. How mortifying, to remember the dear delicious shifts I used to be put to, to gain half a minute's conversation with this fellow! How often have I stole forth, in the coldest night in January, and found him in the garden, stuck like a dripping statue! There would he kneel to me in the snow, and sneeze and cough so pathetically! He shivering with cold and I with apprehension! And while the freezing blasts numbered our joints, how warmly would he press me to pity his flame, and glow with mutual ardour! (*She moves below the sofa, and sits*) Ah, Julia, that was something like being in love!

Julia. If I were in spirits, Lydia, I should chide you only by laughing heartily at you; but it suits more the situation of my mind, at present, earnestly to entreat you not to let a man, who loves you with sincerity, suffer that unhappiness from your caprice, which I know too well caprice can inflict.

(Mrs Malaprop *is heard in great distress off* L. Lydia *rises and runs across* RC. Julia *rises and comes down* C)

Lydia. Oh, Lud! What has brought my aunt here?

(Mrs Malaprop, Fag *and* David *enter* L. Mrs Malaprop *crosses to the sofa and sinks on to it, at the* L *end, very distressed.* Fag *and* David *stand down* L)

Mrs Malaprop. So! So! Here's fine work! Here's fine suicide, paracide, and simulation, going on in the fields! And Sir Anthony not to be found to prevent the antistrophe!

Julia. For Heaven's sake, madam, what's the meaning of this?

Mrs Malaprop. That gentleman can tell you—'twas he enveloped the affair to me.

Lydia (*to Fag*) Do, sir, will you, inform us?

Fag (*coming forward a step*) Ma'am, I should hold myself very deficient in every requisite that forms the man of breeding, if I delayed a moment to give all the information in my power to a lady so deeply interested in the affair as you are.

Lydia. But quick! Quick! sir!

Fag. True, ma'am, as you say, one should be quick in divulging matters of this nature; for should we be tedious, perhaps while we are flourishing on the subject, two or three lives may be lost!

Lydia. Oh, patience! Do, ma'am, for Heaven's sake, tell us what is the matter?

Mrs Malaprop. Why, murder's the matter! Slaughter's the matter! Killing's the matter! But he can tell you the perpendiculars.

Lydia. Then, prithee, sir, be brief.

Fag. Why then, ma'am, as to murder—I cannot take upon me to say—and as to slaughter, or manslaughter, that will be as the jury finds it.

Lydia. But who, sir—who are engaged in this?

Fag. Faith, ma'am, one is a young gentleman whom I should be very sorry anything was to happen to—a very pretty behaved gentleman! We have lived much together, and always on terms.

Lydia. But who is this? Who! Who! Who?

Fag. My master, ma'am—my master—I speak of my master.

Lydia. Heavens! What, Captain Absolute!

Mrs Malaprop (*rising and coming forward a step*) Oh, to be sure, you are frightened now!

Julia. But who are with him, sir?

FAG. As to the rest, ma'am, this gentleman can inform you better than I.

JULIA (*to David*) Do speak, friend.

DAVID (*crossing to R of Fag*) Look'ee, my lady—by the mass!—there's mischief going on. Folks don't use to meet for amusement with firearms, fire-locks, fire-engines, fire-screens, fire-office, and the devil knows what other crackers beside! This, my lady, I say, has an angry favour.

JULIA. But who is there beside Captain Absolute, friend?

DAVID. My poor master—under favour for mentioning him first. You know me, my lady—I am David—and my master of course is, or was, Squire Acres. Then comes Squire Faulkland.

JULIA. Do, ma'am, let us instantly endeavour to prevent mischief.

MRS MALAPROP. Oh fie! It would be very inelegant in us: we should only participate things.

DAVID. Ah, do, Mrs Aunt, save a few lives—they are desperately given, believe me. Above all, there is that bloodthirsty Philistine, Sir Lucius O'Trigger.

MRS MALAPROP. Sir Lucius O'Trigger? (*Going to David*) O mercy! Have they drawn poor little dear Sir Lucius into the scrape? Why, how you stand, girl! You have no more feeling than one of the Derbyshire petrifactions!

LYDIA. What are we to do, madam?

MRS MALAPROP. Why, fly with the utmost felicity, to be sure, to prevent mischief! (*Going to Fag*) Here, friend, you can show us the place?

FAG. If you please, ma'am, I will conduct you. David, do you look for Sir Anthony.

(DAVID *runs off* L)

MRS MALAPROP. Come, girls, this gentleman will exhort us. Come, sir, you're our envoy—lead the way, and we'll precede.

FAG. Not a step before the ladies for the world!

MRS MALAPROP. You're sure you know the spot?

FAG. I think I can find it, ma'am; and one good thing is, we shall hear the report of the pistols as we draw near, so we can't well miss them. Never fear, ma'am, never fear.

(MRS MALAPROP *exits, followed by* LYDIA, JULIA *and* FAG)

SCENE 2

SCENE—*The South Parade.*

CAPTAIN ABSOLUTE *enters* R, *putting his sword under his great-coat.*

ABSOLUTE. A sword seen in the streets of Bath would raise as great an alarm as a mad dog. How provoking this is in Faulkland! Never punctual! I shall be obliged to go without him at last. Oh, the devil! Here's Sir Anthony! How shall I escape him? (*He turns away* R, *and muffles up his face*)

(SIR ANTHONY *enters* L *and crosses to* C. ABSOLUTE *walks past him with deliberate slowness*)

SIR ANTHONY (*as Absolute passes him*) How one may be deceived at a little distance! Only that I see he don't know me, I could have sworn that was Jack!

(ABSOLUTE *stops*)

Hey? (*He goes up to Absolute and turns him*) Gad's life, it is! Why, Jack, what are you afraid of, hey? Sure, I'm right. Why, Jack, Jack Absolute!

ABSOLUTE. Really, sir, you have the advantage of me: I don't remember ever to have had the honour—my name is Saunderson, at your service.

SIR ANTHONY. Sir, I beg your pardon—I took you—hey? Why, zounds!—it is. Stay—(*He pulls the cloak from his face*) So, so—your humble servant, Mr Saunderson? Why, you scoundrel, what tricks are you after now?

ABSOLUTE. Oh, a joke, sir, a joke! I came here on purpose to look for you, sir.

SIR ANTHONY. You did! Well, I am glad you were so lucky. But what are you muffled up for? What's this for? Hey?

ABSOLUTE. 'Tis cool, sir; isn't it? Rather chilly somehow—but I shall be late—(*crossing to* C) I have a particular engagement.

SIR ANTHONY. Stay! Why, I thought you were looking for me? Pray, Jack, where is 't you are going?

ABSOLUTE. Going, sir!

SIR ANTHONY. Ay, where are you going?

ABSOLUTE. Where am I going!

SIR ANTHONY. You unmannerly puppy!

ABSOLUTE. I was going, sir, to—to—to Lydia, sir—to Lydia—to make matters up if I could; and I was looking for you, sir, to—to . . .

SIR ANTHONY. To go with you, I suppose. Well, come along.

ABSOLUTE. Oh zounds! No, sir, not for the world! I wished to meet with you, sir—to—to—to . . . You find it cool, I'm sure, sir—you'd better not stay out.

SIR ANTHONY. Cool? Not at all. Well, Jack—and what will you say to Lydia?

ABSOLUTE. Oh, sir, beg her pardon, humour her—promise and vow. But I detain you, sir—consider the cold air on your gout.

SIR ANTHONY. Oh, not at all! Not at all! I'm in no hurry. Ah! Jack, you youngsters when once you are wounded here (*putting his hand to Captain Absolute's breast*) . . . Hey! What the deuce have you got here?

ABSOLUTE. Nothing, sir—nothing.

SIR ANTHONY. What's this? Here's something d—d hard.

ABSOLUTE. Oh, trinkets, sir! Trinkets! A bauble for Lydia!

SIR ANTHONY. Nay, let me see your taste. (*He pulls his coat open, the sword falls*) Trinkets! A bauble for Lydia! Zounds, sirrah, you are not going to cut her throat, are you?

ABSOLUTE. Ha! Ha! Ha! I thought it would divert you, sir, though I didn't mean to tell you till afterwards.

SIR ANTHONY. You didn't . . . Yes, this is a very diverting trinket, truly!

ABSOLUTE. Sir, I'll explain to you. You know, sir, Lydia is romantic, devilish romantic, and very absurd, of course; now, sir, I intend, if she refuses to forgive me, to unsheath this sword, and swear—I'll fall upon its point, and expire at her feet!

SIR ANTHONY. Fall upon a fiddlestick's end! Why, I suppose it is the very thing that would please her. Get along, you fool!

ABSOLUTE. Well, sir, you shall hear of my success—you shall hear. *Oh, Lydia! Forgive me, or this pointed steel*—says I.

SIR ANTHONY. *Oh, booby! Stab away and welcome*—says she. Get along! And d—n your trinkets!

(ABSOLUTE *exits* L.
    DAVID *enters* R, *running*)

DAVID. Stop him! Stop him! Murder! Thief! Fire! Stop fire! Stop fire! Oh, Sir Anthony—call! Call! Bid 'm stop! Murder! Fire!

SIR ANTHONY. Fire! Murder! Where?

DAVID. Oons! He's out of sight! And I'm out of breath for my part! Oh, Sir Anthony, why didn't you stop him? Why didn't you stop him!

SIR ANTHONY. Zounds! The fellow's mad! Stop whom? Stop Jack?

DAVID. Ay, the captain, sir! There's murder and slaughter . . .

SIR ANTHONY. Murder!

DAVID. Ay, please you, Sir Anthony, there's all kinds of murder, all sorts of slaughter to be seen in the fields: there's fighting going on, sir—bloody sword-and-gun fighting!

SIR ANTHONY. Who are going to fight, dunce?

DAVID. Everybody that I know of, Sir Anthony: everybody is going to fight. My poor master, Sir Lucius O'Trigger, your son, the captain . . .

SIR ANTHONY. Oh, the dog! I see his tricks. Do you know the place?

DAVID. King's-Mead-Fields.

SIR ANTHONY. You know the way?

DAVID. Not an inch: but I'll call the mayor—aldermen—

constables—churchwardens—and beadles—we can't be too many to part them.

Sir Anthony. Come along—give me your shoulder. We'll get assistance as we go. The lying villain! Well, I shall be in such a frenzy! So—this was the history of his trinkets! I'll bauble him!

(Sir Anthony *and* David *exit* l)

Scene 3

Scene—*King's Mead-Fields*

Sir Lucius O'Trigger *enters up* l, *followed by* Acres. *They each carry pistols. They come down* c.

Acres. By my valour, then, Sir Lucius, forty yards is a good distance! Odds levels and aims! I say it is a good distance.

Sir Lucius. It is for muskets or small field-pieces? Upon my conscience, Mr Acres, you must leave these things to me. (*He leads* Acres *across* l, *and places him*) Stay now—I'll show you. (*He measures paces across the stage*) There now, that is a very pretty distance—a pretty gentleman's distance.

Acres. Zounds! We might as well fight in a sentry-box! I tell you, Sir Lucius, the farther he is off, the cooler I shall take my aim.

Sir Lucius (*moving* c) Faith! Then I suppose you would aim at him best of all if he was out of sight!

Acres. No, Sir Lucius; but I should think forty or eight-and-thirty yards . . .

Sir Lucius (*crossing to him*) Pho! Nonsense! Three or four feet between the mouths of your pistols is as good as a mile.

Acres. Odds bullets, no! By my valour! There is no merit in killing him so near: do, my dear Sir Lucius, let me bring him down at a long shot: a long shot, Sir Lucius, if you love me!

Sir Lucius. Well, the gentleman's friend and I must settle that. But tell me now, Mr Acres, in case of an accident, is there any little will or commission I could execute for you?

Acres. I am much obliged to you, Sir Lucius—but I don't understand . . .

Sir Lucius. Why, you may think there's no being shot at without a little risk—and if an unlucky bullet should carry a quietus with it—I say it will be no time then to be bothering you about family matters.

Acres. A quietus!

Sir Lucius. For instance, now—if that should be the case—would you choose to be pickled and sent home? Or would it be the same to you to lie here in the Abbey? I'm told there is a very snug lying in the Abbey.

ACRES. Pickled! Snug lying in the Abbey! Odds tremors! Sir Lucius, don't talk so!

SIR LUCIUS. I suppose, Mr Acres, you never were engaged in an affair of this kind before?

ACRES. No, Sir Lucius, never before.

SIR LUCIUS. Ah! That's a pity! There's nothing like being used to a thing. Pray now, how would you receive the gentleman's shot?

ACRES. Odds files! I've practised that—there, Sir Lucius—(*he stands stiffly, facing front*) there. A side-front, hey? Odd! I'll make myself small enough: I'll stand edgeways.

SIR LUCIUS. Now—you're quite out—for if you stand so when I take my aim . . . (*He retreats to* C, *and levels a pistol at Acres*)

ACRES. Zounds! Sir Lucius—are you sure it is not cock'd?

SIR LUCIUS. Never fear.

ACRES (*backing away* L, *as far as he can*) But—but—you don't know—it may go off of its own head!

SIR LUCIUS. Pho! Be easy. Well, now, if I hit you in the body, my bullet has a double chance—for if it misses a vital part of your right side—'twill be very hard if it don't succeed on the left!

ACRES. A vital part!

SIR LUCIUS (*crossing to Acres and pulling him forward to* LC, *so that he is facing* R) But, there—fix yourself so. Let him see the broadside of your full front—there. Now a ball or two may pass clean through your body, and never do any harm at all.

ACRES. Clean through me! A ball or two clean through me!

SIR LUCIUS. Ay—may they—and it is much the genteelest attitude into the bargain.

ACRES. Look'ee! Sir Lucius—I'd just as lieve be shot in an awkward posture as a genteel one! So, by my valour! I will stand edgeways.

SIR LUCIUS (*looking at his watch*) Sure they don't mean to disappoint us—hah! No, faith—(*looking off,* up L) I think I see them coming.

ACRES. Hey! What! Coming!

SIR LUCIUS. Ay. Who are those yonder getting over the stile!

ACRES (*moving, up* R) There are two of them indeed! Well—let them come. (*He crosses to Sir Lucius, and takes his arm as he leads him down* C) Hey, Sir Lucius! We—we—we—we won't run.

SIR LUCIUS. Run!

ACRES. No—I say—we *won't* run, by my valour!

SIR LUCIUS. What the devil's the matter with you?

ACRES (*crossing to* RC) Nothing—nothing—my dear friend—my dear Sir Lucius—but I—I—I don't feel quite so bold, somehow, as I did.

SIR LUCIUS. Oh fie! Consider your honour.

ACRES. Ay—true—my honour. Do, Sir Lucius, edge in a word or two every now and then about my honour.

Sir Lucius (*looking off* L) Well, here they're coming.

Acres (*moving nervously away* R) Sir Lucius—if I wa'n't with you, I should almost think I was afraid. If my valour should leave me! Valour will come and go.

Sir Lucius (*going to him, and gripping him by the arms*) Then pray keep it fast, while you have it.

Acres. Sir Lucius—I doubt it is going—yes—my valour is certainly going! It is sneaking off! I feel it oozing out as it were at the palms of my hands!

Sir Lucius (*shaking him*) Your honour—your honour! (*He turns away from him to* RC) Here they are.

Acres (*moving farther away* R) Oh mercy! Now—that I was safe at Clod-Hall! Or could be shot before I was aware!

(FAULKLAND *and* CAPTAIN ABSOLUTE *enter up* L. FAULKLAND *comes down* LC, ABSOLUTE *to* C)

Sir Lucius (*bowing*) Gentlemen, your most obedient. Hah! What, Captain Absolute! So, I suppose, sir, you are come here, just like myself—to do a kind office, first for your friend—then to proceed to business on your own account.

Acres (*turning with great joy and surprise*) What, Jack! (*He crosses to him and shakes him by the hand*) My dear Jack! My dear friend!

Absolute. Heark'ee, Bob, Beverley's at hand.

Sir Lucius. Well, Mr Acres—I don't blame your saluting the gentleman civilly. (*To Faulkland*) So, Mr Beverley, if you'll choose your weapons, the captain and I will measure the ground.

Faulkland. *My* weapons, sir!

Acres. Odds life! Sir Lucius, I'm not going to fight Mr Faulkland; these are my particular friends.

Sir Lucius. What, sir, did you not come here to fight Mr Acres?

Faulkland. Not I, upon my word, sir.

Sir Lucius. Well, now, that's mighty provoking! But I hope, Mr Faulkland, as there are three of us come on purpose for the game, you won't be so cantankerous as to spoil the party by sitting out.

Absolute. Oh pray, Faulkland, fight to oblige Sir Lucius.

Faulkland. Nay, if Mr Acres is so bent on the matter . . .

Acres. No, no, Mr Faulkland; I'll bear my disappointment like a Christian. (*Going to Sir Lucius*) Look'ee, Sir Lucius, there's no occasion at all for me to fight; and if it is the same to you, I'd as lieve let it alone.

Sir Lucius. Observe me, Mr Acres—I must not be trifled with. You have certainly challenged somebody—and you came here to fight him. Now, if that gentleman is willing to represent him—I can't see, for my soul, why it isn't just the same thing.

Acres. Why no—Sir Lucius—I tell you, 'tis one Beverley I've challenged—a fellow, you see, that dare not show his face! If *h*. were here, I'd make him give up his pretensions directly.

Absolute (*coming down* c) Hold, Bob—let me set you right—
there is no such man as Beverley in the case. The person who assumed that name is before you; and as his pretensions are the
same in both characters, he is ready to support them in whatever
way you please.

Sir Lucius. Well, this is lucky. Now you have an opportunity . . .

Acres. What, quarrel with my dear friend Jack Absolute?
Not if he were fifty Beverleys! Zounds! Sir Lucius, you would not
have me so unnatural.

Sir Lucius. Upon my conscience, Mr Acres, your valour has
oozed away with a vengeance!

Acres. Not in the least! Odds backs and abettors! I'll be your
second with all my heart—and if you should get a *quietus*, you
may command me entirely. I'll get you *snug lying* in the *Abbey
here;* or pickle you, and send you over to Blunderbuss-Hall, or
anything of the kind, with the greatest pleasure.

Sir Lucius. Pho! Pho! You are little better than a coward.

Acres. Mind, gentlemen, he calls me a *coward;* coward was
the word, by my valour!

Sir Lucius. Well, sir?

Acres. Look'ee, Sir Lucius, 'tisn't that I mind the word
coward—*coward* may be said in a joke. But if you had called me a
poltroon, odds daggers and balls . . .

Sir Lucius. Well, sir?

Acres. I should have thought you a very ill-bred man.

Sir Lucius (*turning away down* R) Pho! You are beneath my
notice.

Absolute. Nay, Sir Lucius, you can't have a better second
than my friend Acres. He is a most *determined dog*—called in the
country, *Fighting Bob*. He generally *kills a man a week*—don't you,
Bob?

Acres. Ay—at home!

Sir Lucius. Well, then, Captain, 'tis we must begin—so come
out, my little counsellor—(*he draws his sword*)

(Acres *backs away up* R *and edges round and down stage* R)

—and ask the gentleman, whether he will resign the lady, without
forcing you to proceed against him?

Absolute. Come on then, sir. (*He draws*) Since you won't let
it be an amicable suit, here's my reply.

(Sir Lucius *and* Absolute *throw themselves into attitudes of
combat.*
      David *enters up* L *followed by* Sir Anthony, Lydia, Mrs
Malaprop *and* Julia. David *crosses up* RC. Sir Anthony *comes
down* C, *and knocks up the swords.* Lydia, Mrs Malaprop *and*
Julia *remain up* L)

DAVID. Knock 'em all down, sweet Sir Anthony; knock down my master in particular; and bind his hands over to their good behaviour!

SIR ANTHONY. Put up, Jack, put up, or I shall be in a frenzy —how came you in a duel, sir?

(SIR LUCIUS *and* ABSOLUTE *slip back. The former going up* R, *the latter to* LC. FAULKLAND *moves down* L)

ABSOLUTE. Faith, sir, that gentleman can tell you better than I; 'twas he called on me, and you know, sir, I serve his majesty.

SIR ANTHONY. Here's a pretty fellow; I catch him going to cut a man's throat, and he tells me, he serves his majesty! Zounds! Sirrah, then how durst you draw the king's sword against one of his subjects?

ABSOLUTE. Sir! I tell you, that gentleman called me out, without explaining his reasons.

SIR ANTHONY. Gad, sir! How came you to call my son out, without explaining your reasons?

SIR LUCIUS. Your son, sir, insulted me in a manner which my honour could not brook.

SIR ANTHONY. Zounds! Jack, how durst thou insult the gentleman in a manner which his honour could not brook?

(ABSOLUTE *resentfully moves* L. FAULKLAND *moves disconsolately still farther down* L

MRS MALAPROP *comes down* C *to* L *of* SIR ANTHONY. LYDIA *follows her down and stands* L *of her*)

MRS MALAPROP. Come, come, let's have no honour before ladies. Captain Absolute, come here.

(ABSOLUTE *turns and moves towards Lydia*)

How could you intimidate us so? Here's Lydia has been terrified to death for you.

ABSOLUTE. For fear I should be killed, or escape, ma'am?

MRS MALAPROP. Nay, no delusions to the past. Lydia is convinced; speak, child.

SIR LUCIUS (*coming down to Lydia*) With your leave, ma'am, I must put in a word here; I believe I could interpret the young lady's silence. Now mark . . .

LYDIA. What is it you mean, sir?

(MRS MALAPROP *moves behind Lydia to* LC)

SIR LUCIUS. Come, come, Delia, we must be serious now—this is no time for trifling.

LYDIA. 'Tis true, sir; and your reproof bids me offer this gentleman my hand, and solicit the return of his affections.

ABSOLUTE (*going to Lydia*) Oh, my little angel! Say you so! Sir Lucius—I perceive there must be some mistake here, with regard to the affront which you affirm I have given you. I can only say, that it could not have been intentional. And as you must be convinced that I should not fear to support a real injury, you shall now see that I am not ashamed to atone for an inadvertency —I ask your pardon. But for this lady, while honoured with her approbation, I will support my claim against any man whatever.

SIR ANTHONY. Well said, Jack, and I'll stand by you, my boy. (*He moves away down* R)

ACRES (*crossing to* RC) Mind, I give up all my claim. I make no pretensions to anything in the world; and if I can't get a wife without fighting for her—by my valour, I'll live a bachelor! (*He turns away up* RC)

(ABSOLUTE *crosses* Lydia *to Sir Lucius*)

SIR LUCIUS. Captain, give me your hand: an affront handsomely acknowledged becomes an obligation; and as for the lady, if she chooses to deny her own handwriting, here . . . (*He takes out some letters*)

MRS MALAPROP. Oh, he will dissolve my mystery! (*Crossing to* R *of Sir Lucius*) Sir Lucius, perhaps there's some mistake—perhaps I can illuminate . . .

SIR LUCIUS. Pray, old gentlewoman, don't interfere where you have no business. (*Turning to Lydia*) Miss Languish, are you my Delia, or not?

LYDIA. Indeed, Sir Lucius, I am not. (*She turns to Absolute*)

(ABSOLUTE *and* LYDIA *walk round* L, *up stage and across to Acres*)

MRS MALAPROP. Sir Lucius O'Trigger—ungrateful as you are —I own the soft impeachment—pardon my blushes—I am Delia.

SIR LUCIUS. You, Delia? Pho! Pho! Be easy!

MRS MALAPROP. Why, thou barbarous Vandyke! Those letters are mine. When you are more sensible of my benignity—perhaps I may be brought to encourage your addresses.

SIR LUCIUS. Mrs Malaprop, I am extremely sensible of your condescension; and whether you or Lucy have put this trick upon me, I am equally beholden to you. And, to show you I am not ungrateful, (*moving away to* LC *and turning*) Captain Absolute, since you have taken that lady from me, I'll give you my Delia into the bargain.

ABSOLUTE. I am much obliged to you, Sir Lucius; but here's my friend, Fighting Bob, unprovided for.

SIR LUCIUS. Hah! Little Valour—(*indicating Mrs Malaprop*) here, will you make your fortune?

ACRES. Odds wrinkles! No. (*Crossing to Sir Lucius*) But give me your hand, Sir Lucius, forget and forgive; but if ever I give you a chance of *pickling* me again, say Bob Acres is a dunce, that's all.

SIR ANTHONY (*crossing to Mrs Malaprop*) Come, Mrs Malaprop, don't be cast down—you are in your bloom yet

Mrs Malaprop. Oh, Sir Anthony—men are all barbarians.

(Sir Anthony *and* Mrs Malaprop *turn and move up* c.
Absolute *and* Lydia *move up* r. Sir Lucius *and* Acres *join them.*
Julia *comes forward to* c)

Julia (*aside*) He seems dejected and unhappy—not sullen;
there was some foundation, however, for the tale he told me.
Oh, woman, how true should be your judgement, when your
resolution is so weak!

(Faulkland *turns as though to go up* l. *He sees Julia, stops, and
moves towards her*)

Faulkland. Julia—how can I sue for what I so little deserve?
I dare not presume—yet Hope is the child of Penitence.
Julia. Oh, Faulkland, you have been more faulty in your
unkind treatment of me, than I am now in wanting inclination
to resent it. As my heart honestly bids me place my weakness
to the account of love, I should be ungenerous not to admit the
same plea for yours.
Faulkland. Now I shall be blest indeed!
Sir Anthony (*coming forward to* r *of Julia*) What's going on
here? So you have been quarrelling, too, I warrant! Come, Julia,
I never interfered before; but let me have a hand in the matter
at last. All the faults I have ever seen in my friend Faulkland
seemed to proceed from what he calls the *delicacy* and *warmth* of
his affection for you. There, marry him directly, Julia; you'll find
he'll mend surprisingly.

(Absolute *and* Lydia *come down* rc. Sir Lucius *and* Acres
come down r. Mrs Malaprop *comes down* l *of Faulkland*)

Sir Lucius. Come, now, I hope there is no dissatisfied person
but what is content; for as I have been disappointed myself, it
will be very hard if I have not the satisfaction of seeing other
people succeed better.
Acres. You are right, Sir Lucius. (*Shaking hands with* Absolute)
So, Jack, I wish you joy. (*Crossing to* r *of Faulkland*) Mr Faulkland,
the same. (*He turns up stage between Julia and Lydia, taking each by
the arm and leading them up* c *a little way*)

(Julia *and* Lydia *move slightly above Sir Anthony.* Sir Anthony
goes r *a little*)

Ladies—come now, to show you I'm neither vexed nor angry,
odds tabors and pipes! I'll order the fiddles in half an hour to the
New Rooms—and I insist on your all meeting me there.
Sir Anthony (*following Acres*) 'Gad, sir! I like your spirit; and
at night we single lads will drink a health to the young couples,
and a husband to Mrs Malaprop.
Faulkland. Our partners are stolen from us, Jack—I hope to

be congratulated by each other—*yours* for having checked in time the errors of an ill-directed imagination, which might have betrayed an innocent heart; and *mine,* for having, by her gentleness and candour, reformed the unhappy temper of one, who by it made wretched whom he loved most, and tortured the heart he ought to have adored.

ABSOLUTE. Well, Faulkland, we have both tasted the bitters, as well as the sweets of love; with the difference only, that *you* always prepared the bitter cup for yourself, while I . . .

(LYDIA *and* JULIA *come down, deliberately separating Absolute and Faulkland, as they come between them*)

LYDIA. Was always obliged to *me* for it, hey, Mr Modesty? But, come no more of that—our happiness is now as unalloyed as general.

(SIR ANTHONY *moves to Mrs Malaprop*)

JULIA. Then let us study to preserve it so: and while Hope pictures to us a flattering scene of future bliss, let us deny its pencil those colours which are too bright to be lasting. (*Coming forward to the audience*) When hearts deserving happiness would unite their fortunes, Virtue would crown them with an unfading garland of modest hurtless flowers; but ill-judging Passion will force the gaudier rose into the wreath, whose thorns offend them when its leaves are dropt!

CURTAIN

FURNITURE AND PROPERTY PLOT

ACT I

SCENE 1

Whip (COACHMAN)

SCENE 2

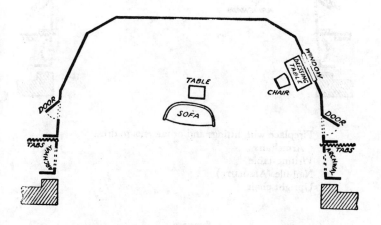

Sofa with cushions
Table. *On it:* six books
Dressing-table. *On it:* standing mirror, smelling-salts, books, toilet set
Chair
List of transactions (LUCY)
Silver-mounted cane (SIR ANTHONY)
　(The cane is carried throughout the play)

ACT II

SCENE 1

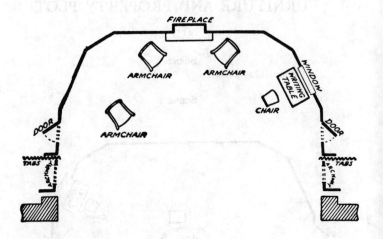

Fireplace with fittings and ornaments to dress
3 Armchairs
Writing-table
Nail-file (ABSOLUTE)
Upright chair

SCENE 2

Letter (LUCY)
Cane, money (SIR LUCIUS)
    (The cane is carried throughout the play)

ACT III

SCENE 1

None

SCENE 2

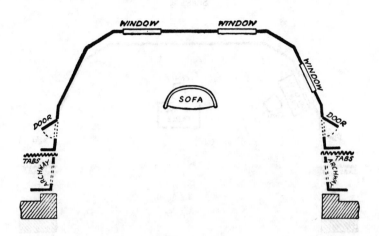

Sofa with cushions

SCENE 3

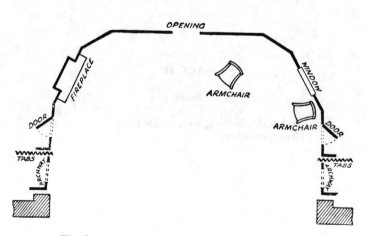

Fireplace
2 Armchairs
Letter (MRS MALAPROP)

SCENE 4

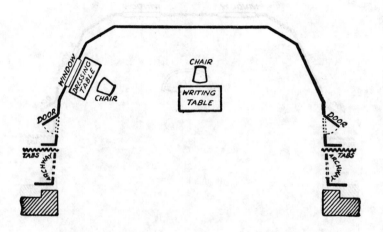

Dressing-table. *On it:* mirror, toilet set, peruke block
Writing-table. *On it:* writing materials, sealing-wax, candle
2 Chairs

ACT IV

SCENE I

As Act III, Scene 4, with candle alight
Cane (ABSOLUTE)

SCENE 2

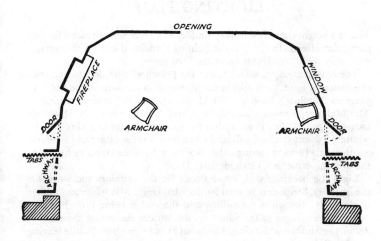

As Act III, Scene 3
Miniature (LYDIA)
Miniature (ABSOLUTE)

SCENE 3
Letter (SERVANT)

ACT V

SCENE 1
As Act III, Scene 2
Letter (JULIA)

SCENE 2
None

SCENE 3
Pistols (ACRES and SIR LUCIUS)
Letter (SIR LUCIUS)

LIGHTING PLOT

This is a bright comedy and very simple, and there is no demand for any particular effects. In general the lighting remains the same throughout with only slight modifications in the final scene.

The acting areas, C, R and L, are the principal ones demanding concentration of light, with additional attention to the area round the fireplace in Absolute's lodging (Act II, Sc. 1), and the centre opening in Mrs Malaprop's room (Act III, Sc. 3 and Act IV, Sc. 2). In Absolute's lodgings (Act II, Sc. 1) an additional spot can be trained through the window L so as to strike Faulkland when he sits at the table; and similarly another can be used through the window R to strike Acres as he sits at the dressing-table in his lodging (Act III, Sc. 4)

Light the backings with white floods for the exteriors and straw for the interiors. Strips can be used for door backings. Mix white and amber in the floats, the white prevailing, and the amber being brought up to soften the harshness of the white. In the battens the amber should predominate, and the white should be brought in to give body, while leaving a softer light than is obtained from the floats.

The final scene of the play takes place in the evening. Soften the light a little by taking down the white circuits in both floats and battens, and use straws or pale amber in offstage floods. Pick out the C, R and L acting areas with widespread spots so that the characters are not obscured.

EDITOR'S NOTE

The settings have been designed to provide a simple and adaptable mounting for the play, requiring only small readjustments for the different scenes. They also enable the action to take place in elementary curtains if necessary (two pairs for wings, and one pair for the back-cloth) without interfering with the movements as planned. Incidentally these movements have been based on the traditional ones as shown in early copies of the play, to which others have been added where required. As so many examples of eighteenth-century architecture are in existence, it should be quite easy to supplement the decorative features of the period—pillasters, panel, mouldings, etc. If scenery is not available, the final scene of the play can be played in green curtains, with entrances up R and up L.

Passages usually omitted in production are shown between square brakets [ ].